AF264341

Ancient China

Discovering Lost Stories from Chinese History

Free Bonus from Captivating History
(Available for a Limited time)

Hi History Lovers!

Now you have a chance to join our exclusive history list so you can get your first history ebook for free as well as discounts and a potential to get more history books for free!

Simply visit the link below to join.

Or, Scan the QR code!

captivatinghistory.com/ebook

Also, make sure to follow us on Facebook, X, and YouTube by searching for Captivating History.

Table of Contents

Introduction

Speaking of the world's oldest and earliest civilizations, our minds cannot help but wander to the ancient Egyptians under god-like pharaohs, the battles fought by the Spartans, and of course, the cuneiform and ziggurats once built by the Sumerians. The Chinese civilization, however, began later—about 1,500 years after the rise of Egypt and Sumer. But China also belongs to another category: the world's oldest continuous civilization. For over four thousand years, the Chinese civilization had witnessed the birth of dynasties and their declines, philosophies blossoming and waning, and different inventions that reshaped the world. And yet, it endured. The continuity of its language, traditions, and recorded history distinguishes it from every other ancient culture.

Just like any other civilization's, China's history is layered. At first there were myths and legends that spoke about the civilization's beginnings. These stories include tales of the sage kings (Yao, Shun, and Yu) who were often credited with introducing agriculture to the people, instituting moral rule, and even taming rivers and floods that endangered the land and its inhabitants. Then, the story moved into firmer ground, complete with archaeological evidence and written records. This is when the timeline begins to sharpen.

Both archaeology and contemporary records firmly attest that the Shang dynasty (c. 1600–1046 BCE) is the very first Chinese dynasty. The discovery of the oracle bones, in particular, gives us a glimpse into its world of kingship, warfare, and ancestor worship. Its capital was at Anyang. This was where palaces once stood with the royal tombs telling us much more about the foundations of early Chinese statecraft. After the Shang came the Zhou dynasty (c. 1046-256 BCE), which developed the idea of the Mandate of Heaven. This doctrine justified a ruler's authority as divinely granted. The mandate could be revoked, however, if he governed poorly. This idea would shape Chinese political thought for many centuries to come.

The later periods of Zhou, especially the Spring and Autumn (770-476 BCE) and the Warring States (475-221 BCE) periods, saw thinkers including Confucius, Laozi, and Mozi rise to prominence. Indeed, the Zhou era is remembered as the cradle of Chinese philosophy. But at the same time, it was an age of endless wars and violence. Chaos only ended—at least for a while—when Qin Shi Huang united the states, becoming China's first emperor and kickstarting the Qin dynasty (221-206 BCE).

After the short-lived Qin dynasty came the Han dynasty (206 BCE-220 CE), which took the kingdom to greater heights. It expanded territory, opened the Silk Road to Central Asia, and developed a sophisticated bureaucracy grounded in Confucian ideals. These achievements are preserved in ancient texts such as the *Shiji* (Records of the Grand Historian), and the *Hanshu* (Book of Han), both of which were compiled by great historians of that age. These accounts also provided us with vivid portraits of emperors, generals, scholars, and insights into everyday life. These works, along with later dynastic histories, were undoubtedly crucial sources for reconstructing the past and will often appear in the chapters that follow.

When the Han faltered, China entered a period of fragmentation once more. This long interlude of division only came to an end with the rise of the Sui dynasty (581-618 CE). Succeeding it was none other than the Tang dynasty (618-907 CE), which is often described by historians and scholars as the Golden Age of Chinese civilization. Here, the Chinese empire reached its zenith. Its borders were expanded even more, giving way for the civilization's ideas to spread across Eurasia and Chinese goods to travel along the Silk Road. Even poetry and literature reached greater heights with figures like Li Bai and Du Fu rising to prominence. Though some historians classify the Tang as part of medieval rather than ancient China, its cultural achievements and global influence ensure its place as one of the crowning moments of China's early history.

To cover the entire history of China would probably take endless pages. The civilization's story is so long that many stories within it have been nearly forgotten. And so, this book aims not to retell the parts that are already widely known but rather to focus on the voices and episodes that have slipped through the cracks of grand narratives.

Chapter 1 – Forgotten and Vanished

Some consider the Taklamakan Desert one of the most isolated locations on earth. The desert was known as the place of no return, and this was for a reason. This deadly sea of sand stretches across northwestern China for more than 330,000 square kilometers. Named one of the largest shifting-sand deserts in the world, the region consists of nothing but vast dunes that rise and fall like waves on a frozen ocean. Believe it or not, some can tower as high as three hundred meters! Since the winds reshape the landscape almost constantly, you could easily get lost; the wind would erase your footprints and swallow your paths within hours if not minutes. The desert is even deadlier in the summer months. Surface temperatures can climb to blistering extremes. But winter is no better: the nights are usually ice cold with temperatures dropping well below freezing. Unsurprisingly, water is hard to come by. Those who are brave enough to traverse across it risk death by thirst and disorientation. Even if you survive thirst, the sudden sandstorms could easily bury you alive.

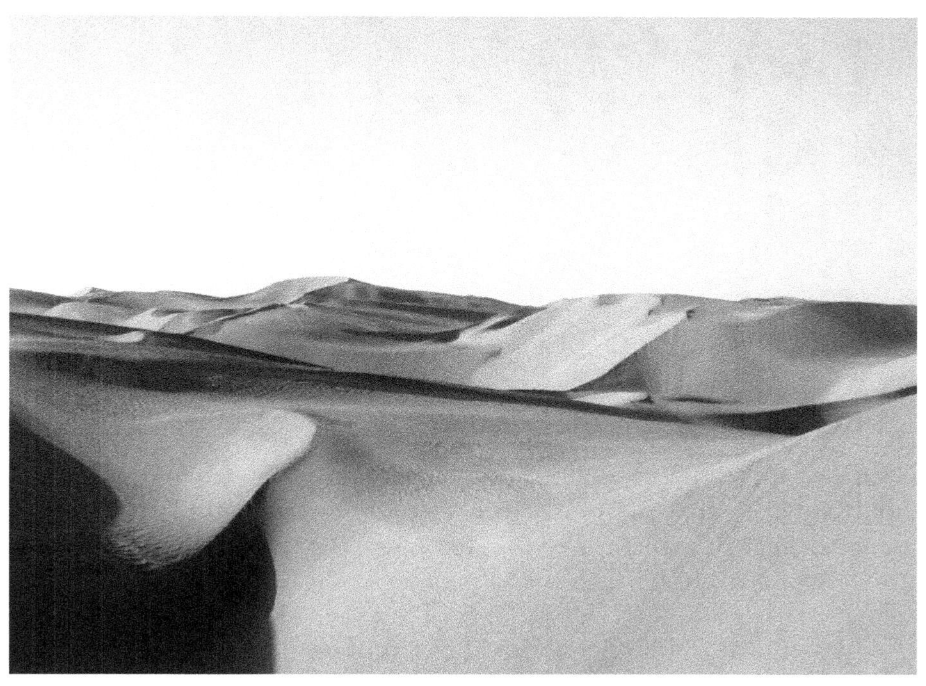

The Tamaklan Desert.[1]

It is no wonder that during ancient times, caravans traveling along the Silk Road preferred to avoid traversing the secluded desert. Typically, ancient merchants would choose one of the two safer paths that would take them around the edges of Taklamakan. The northern route followed the line of the Tianshan Mountains, skirting the desert's rim through a string of oases before heading westward. The southern route, however, required merchants to trace the foothills of the Kunlun Mountains, which would eventually lead them to settlements that clung to rivers flowing down from the highlands. Both routes eventually rejoined on the far side of the Tarim Basin. This allowed the ancient merchants to continue their journey toward Central Asia and beyond.

However, before pressing onward, some would stop at a certain oasis kingdom to replenish their supplies, trade their goods, and rest their animals. Known as Loulan, this fortified city sat on the eastern edge of the Tarim Basin near the salt lake of Lop Nur (also known as Luóbù Pō). Mud-brick houses dotted the city, with fields of millet and barley adorning its landscape. To weary travelers, the sight of this city and its canals carrying water from the Tarim must have appeared like a mirage turned real.

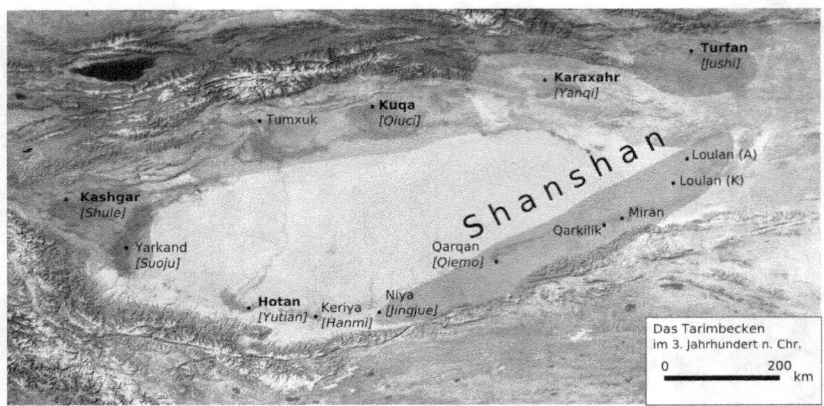

The Tarim Basin and its surrounding areas, circa 3rd century.[2]

One of the earliest mentions of Loulan came from its conquerors. In 126 BCE, the Chanyu, supreme leader of the Xiongnu, wrote to the Han emperor. In his letter, he boasted his victories, claiming that he had subdued an array of territories and people, from the nomadic pastoralists Yuezhi to the Wusun, the Jie, and of course, the Loulan. While the letter was meant to intimidate the Han emperor, the mention of Loulan also placed the city on the pedestal of history, turning it into a political prize that both the Xiongnu and the Han would compete to control in the centuries that followed.

Another mention came from a traveler named Zhang Qian, who was dispatched the same year by the Han dynasty. His mission was to cross the Tarim Basin, initiate transcontinental trade on the Silk Road, and seek alliances in the Western regions to join their fight against the Xiongnu. Zhang Qian passed by Lop Nur and laid eyes on Loulan. According to his description, the city was unlike any other settlement in the desert. Not only did it have walls that guarded the fields and canals that sustained it, but its location was also strategic: Loulan stood at the crossroads of east and west. The reports of his travels were so valuable that even Sima Qian quoted them extensively in his chronicles.

Unfortunately, it was its strategic location that invited chaos. The Han dynasty had its eyes on the city, aiming to turn Loulan into a buffer and staging post for the Silk Road. The Xiongnu, on the other hand, planned to transform it into a forward base against Han advances. Eventually, both sides pressed the city to swear loyalty. The Han, for instance, sent more envoys into the western regions after Zhang Qian returned with his reports. But the desert was relentless, and its inhabitants too were fierce. Historical records, especially from the Book of Han, recalled how

Loulan and its neighbor, Gushi, laid an attack against the Han envoys. When news of the assault reached the Han court, more troops were dispatched, with the goal of subduing Loulan and forcing it to pay tribute. Unable to face such massive and powerful forces, Loulan relented.

Of course, the Xiongnu also refused to remain silent. After all, they had already boasted their grip over the city in a letter to the Han. They, too, demanded tribute. Loulan was forced to hand over grain and livestock to their court, as well. The kingdom was now caught between the two powers. Loulan knew that to defy one of them would certainly bring destruction. Even hostages (princes) were handed to these powers. It was only when a Loulan king died that the hostages were allowed to return home. The new king, however, was required to send his own sons in their place.

Tensions finally broke out when a prince raised in the Xiongnu court ascended as the new king of Loulan. The Han emperor demanded that the new king present himself to demonstrate allegiance. However, the Loulan king refused to do so. This was largely due to the Han breaking their promise: they had failed to return one of the hostages when the new Loulan king ascended the throne. The Loulan also grew bolder and began attacking Han envoys once more.

What followed was violence. The Han emperor sent an emissary named Fu Jiezi to the city. He traveled to Loulan with all sorts of goods, including silk, gold, and fine wine. The king welcomed the envoy with open arms and held a feast for him. Fu Jiezi then presented his fine wine and offered to pour the king a drink, to which he gladly accepted. Fu Jiezi made sure he refilled the king's goblet each time he drank the wine. When the king was finally drunk, Fu Jiezi stabbed him to death. His severed head was then hung from one of Loulan's towers as a warning to those who dared to resist the "Son of Heaven."

This marked the end of Loulan's independence. A new king indeed rose to the Loulan throne—the younger brother of the assassinated king—but he was nothing more than a puppet of the Han. The kingdom also received a new name. Referred to as Shanshan, the kingdom was forever bound to the empire of the east.

Although its sovereignty was a thing of the past, the oasis city was still a hot spot for caravans traveling through the desert. In fact, Loulan remained a vital link in the Silk Road network. Archaeological findings reveal a culture both practical and cosmopolitan. Textiles dyed in reds and blues speak of local skill. Tools, combs, and pottery show everyday adaptation to desert life.

But still, prosperity was not meant to last; it was as fragile as the waters that sustained the city. As centuries passed, the Tarim River shifted its course. It no longer flowed reliably into Lop Nur. With its water supply depleting and its canals slowly cracking into empty ditches, Loulan began to falter. Its decline was also hastened by the raids launched by many nomadic tribes in the region. Then came the shifting of the trade routes, which led to Loulan's further decay. The Buddhist pilgrim, Faxian, who passed through the city during his travels in 399 CE, wrote how the city had become a ghost town, waiting for the sands to eventually swallow it whole.

Loulan was consumed by both the towering sands and time itself. It was only in 1900 that the kingdom resurfaced when a Swedish adventurer named Sven Hedin stumbled across the ruins as he journeyed through the Tarim Basin. There, he found what was left of the once flourishing oasis city: remnants of the sun-dried brick walls that protected the people and their fields thousands of years ago, destroyed watchtowers, and the dry bed of a canal that once fed the oasis.

After Hedin came the Hungarian British archaeologist Aurel Stein, who studied the site and documented it in detail. Excavations revealed a variety of artifacts such as coins, official documents, silk fabrics, lacquerware, wood carvings, and bronze tools. Some of these items even show Greco-Roman influences. These discoveries undoubtedly confirmed Loulan's life as a Silk Road city.

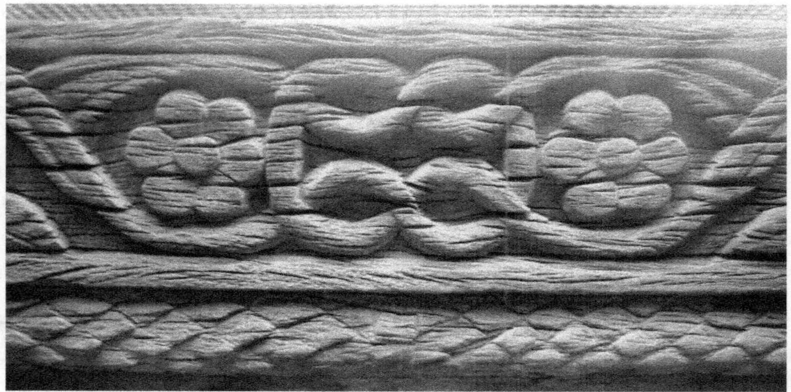

A carved wooden beam recovered from Loulan, which bore patterns influenced by ancient Western civilizations.[3]

One of the two most remarkable discoveries was the underground water channels, which were similar to the *karez* systems still used today by the peoples of the region—particularly the Uyghurs. Relying on differences in altitude and the pull of gravity, these water channels could collect meltwater from distant mountains and guide it toward the oasis. Since the channels were built underground, water was protected from both sandstorms and the desert sun.

Of course, Buddhism too left its mark on the vanished kingdom. Along with modest houses, temples and pagodas were also uncovered from the sands. These structures are evidence of the spread of the Buddhist faith across the desert by the first centuries CE. Scholars suggest that Loulan may have been a rest stop for monks and pilgrims who were traveling between China and India.

The second most remarkable finding was the body of a woman, referred to by historians as the Loulan Beauty. This mummy was discovered in 1980. Although tests showed that she lived nearly four thousand years prior to the kingdom's height, it is hard to dismiss the exceptional state of her body. Preserved perfectly by the desert's temperature and arid air, the mummy still has auburn hair attached to its skull. Even some of her delicate features survived the test of time—as if she was buried only a few decades ago.

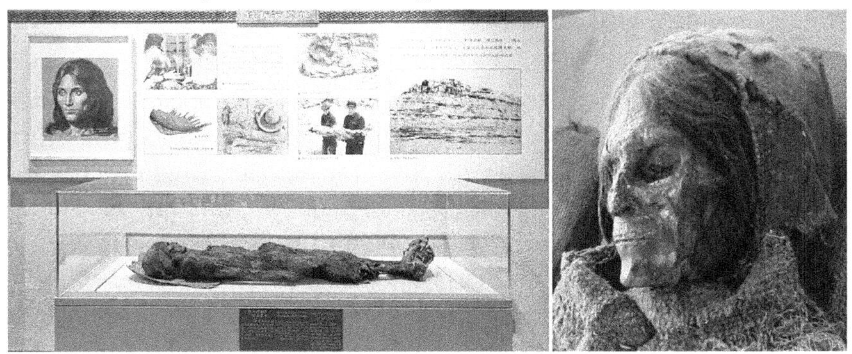

The Beauty of Loulan, now exhibited at Xinjian Museum.'

Today, the site of Loulan lies within a restricted military zone. While its ruins are largely inaccessible, its story continues to captivate historians and archaeologists.

A Discovery That Challenged China's Well-Known Past

The *Iliad* is thought to have been composed by Homer in the seventh or eighth century BCE. It narrates the Trojan War, which revolved around the ancient city of Troy. Although the Trojan War became a favorite subject, especially in the history of ancient Greece, many dismissed the city's existence as pure myth. This view, however, changed in the 1870s.

German archaeologist Heinrich Schliemann, convinced that the city was real, embarked on a mission to uncover the truth. Arriving at the hills of Hisarlik in modern-day Turkey, he dug layer by layer until he eventually uncovered the stone walls and artifacts of a city long thought to be imaginary. From then on, Troy was no longer the stuff of poetry alone. It was real, complex, and historical. Its rediscovery undoubtedly reset the way the world thought about ancient Greece.

Then, over a century later, something very similar happened in China. For many years, it was common belief that all Chinese civilization began in a single place—the fertile valley of the Yellow River. It was here that many dynasties rose in sequence, starting from the mysterious Xia to the Shang and Zhou, who each built upon the achievements of the dynasty before. Archaeology confirmed much of this story. The Shang dynasty, which centered at Anyang, left plenty of evidence for our generation to uncover, such as the oracle bones (the earliest Chinese writing, used for divination) and ritual bronzes, which were believed to have been commonly used in ancestor worship. Meanwhile, other regions like Sichuan, Yunnan, or the south were seen as peripheral; they borrowed culture and influence from the Shang and were never considered equal centers of civilization in their own right.

Fast forward to the early twentieth century when historians saw the need to redraw the map of China's past. It all began with a certain farmer named Yan Daochang. In 1929, the farmer accidentally made an astonishing discovery while he was digging a well in his field in Guanghan, Sichuan. As it turns out, beneath his land was a large stash of jade artifacts. Excavations took place for decades following this discovery, but the finds did not cause much of a stir. Jade is indeed valuable, but since the gemstone fit within the broad traditions of Chinese antiquity, these discoveries were not considered unusual.

Another discovery in 1986, however, appeared strange enough that it challenged everything historians thought they knew about the origins of Chinese civilization. Archaeologists had uncovered two enormous sacrificial pits. Expecting yet another cache of jade, they were surprised to learn that beneath the earth was a bronze mask with features they had never seen before. Its almond-shaped eyes bulged outward; the nose was sharp and protruding, while the ears flared wide. These features were utterly unlike anything in the Chinese Bronze Age. This was not the only mask they uncovered. They also found one inlaid with gold foil and a few others that varied in size but were similar in fashion.

As days passed, more artifacts surfaced. One of the most popular was a standing bronze man that measured at least eight feet tall. It featured a long pair of arms that made it appear as if the statue was presenting a gift to the heavens above. Historians suggest it could be plausible that in its glory days, the statue once held a sacred object, perhaps a piece an ornament of jade or ivory.

The same year, hundreds of broken pieces of a bronze tree were uncovered. Upon restoration (which took nearly a decade to complete), the sacred tree appeared rather massive. The trunk itself rose in three tiers, each featuring three branches growing out of it. Curling downward like flowing ribbons, these branches also had flowers at full bloom, complete with small birds perched on top of them. From these larger branches sprouted smaller offshoots, each heavy with fruit. In total, there were twenty-seven

The reconstructed Sanxingdui sacred tree.[5]

of them, glimmering like a treasure left under the blazing sun. Last but not least, the sacred tree also has a dragon twining around its lower trunk. The artistry was surreal, especially considering it was constructed many thousands of years ago.

Other treasures found buried underneath the earth included elephant tusks, gold scepters, jade blades, cowrie shells, and ritual vessels. To many, these items may look like the refuse of a city, but to well-trained eyes, they could be a part of a massive ritual deposit on a scale unlike anything known from the Shang.

Historians familiar with the culture of the Shang dynasty could easily notice the stark contrast. While the geometrical bronze vessels from the Shang were typically heavy, symmetrical, and decorated with *taotie* motifs, the ones from the Sanxingdui site were completely different; most of them took on fantastical and sculptural forms. It's also possibly their purpose was not the same. While bronzes from the Shang dynasty were linked to ritual feasting and ancestor worship, the ones from Sanxingdui appear to have been part of sacrificial pits. Many Sanxingdui artifacts were deliberately broken or burned before burial, which could suggest a very distinct set of religious beliefs.

Remarkably, the earth had not finished giving up its treasures. Excavations in 2021 resulted in the discovery of six more sacrificial pits, all full of mysterious artifacts. Another bronze mask was uncovered, though this one was larger than the archaeologists had ever seen. Dating to around 1300–1100 BCE, the mask was over seventy centimeters high and 131 centimeters wide. It was so massive that its face, eyes, and ears had been cast separately before being soldered together. It also had openings on the forehead and at the sides that led archaeologists to believe that it was once attached to something else—perhaps a great statue or a wooden effigy. Upon further inspection, archaeologists also found traces of silk near the mask's right eye. The reason for this is still being discussed.

Apart from the big bronze mask, a rather peculiar figure was also uncovered from another one of the pits. Rising to seventy-five centimeters tall, this statue was a hybrid of a tiger and a dragon. It featured a pair of bulging eyes, a set of jutting teeth, and a band-like piece in its mouth. On its base stood a bird.

In light of these discoveries, it is safe to assume that the Sanxingdui culture was not an offshoot of Shang culture but an independent civilization equal in sophistication, with its own worldview.

Soon, archaeologists pointed to the ancient Shu culture, arriving at a plausible conclusion that Sanxingdui was connected to it. Indeed, Shu had been mentioned in later Chinese texts, but its history was murky and often shrouded in legend and myths. Its first king was believed to be an individual named Cancong, who was credited with introducing significant advancements in agriculture and silk production. King Cancong of Shu was also said to have had bulging eyes. Scholars suggest that his unique feature marked him as more than just a mortal king. Perhaps, to his people, he may have been seen as a shaman or even a divine figure. Interestingly, this belief seemed to echo uncannily in the Sanxingdui masks, which often sport the same protruding eyes.

The bronze mask, thought to be a depiction of King Cancong.[6]

For centuries, Shu was considered peripheral to the grand dynasties of the north, if it was considered at all. But Sanxingdui changed that view. What's more, the civilization's discovery also reset assumptions about early China entirely. It was no longer possible to view Chinese civilization as flowing from a single source in the Yellow River Valley. Archaeological evidence proved that China's Bronze Age had multiple centers that flourished in their own ways. The Shang dynasty shone in the north, while Sanxingdui rose in Sichuan.

However, just as suddenly as it appeared, Sanxingdui vanished. The site was abandoned sometime around 1100 BCE, leaving behind zero written texts to explain the reasons. But, of course, theories abound. Geologists suggest that the region was struck by a massive earthquake. This shifted the flow of the Min River, cutting off water to the city. Without water, life in the Sichuan basin would have been impossible.

Hence, the population was left with no other choice but to move. Another theory involves catastrophic flooding, which was hinted at in ancient texts. If this was true, the flood could have drowned the city. The burned artifacts in the pits might have been part of desperate rituals to appease the gods and stop a catastrophic event.

Invasion could also be one of the reasons the culture suddenly vanished. Sanxingdui was rich in gold and bronze, making it a tempting prize for neighboring, power-hungry rivals. If an enemy overran the city, the ritual destruction of sacred objects could have been intended to break the enemy's spiritual power.

A golden mask uncovered from Jinsha, which had details similar to those from Sanxingdui.[7]

The most intriguing theory, however, comes from just forty kilometers away, at the site Jinsha (located in Qinyang, Sichuan). Here, archaeologists had uncovered another collection of artifacts that bore a striking resemblance to those unearthed at Guanghan. This included bronze and gold masks—though they were smaller than the ones found in Guanghan—jade, and ivory. These findings suggest that the Sanxingdui simply relocated, turning Jinsha into their new center. If so, Sanxingdui did not vanish entirely but lived on in a new landscape.

Chapter 2 – Unsung Men of Ancient China

It was 383 CE, and the balance of power in China appeared hopelessly uneven. A battle was about to take place on the banks of the Fei River (located in present-day Anhui Province). On one side stood the forces of the Former Qin, who were fighting for their ambitious ruler, Fu Jian. According to ancient chroniclers, Fu Jian had dispatched nearly 900,000 men, whom he had gathered from every corner of his empire.

Camping across the water were only 80,000 soldiers of the smaller Eastern Jin dynasty. The sight of their enemy must have been overwhelming. The Qin outnumbered them well over ten to one. Their camp stretched as far as the eye could see. When night came, fires from their camp dotted the night sky as if the constellations themselves had come down to earth. The neighing of countless horses, which echoed day and night, added tension to the air. For a time, it looked like the heavenly gods themselves had already decided the victor of the battle.

Yet, the forces of Jin were not so easily deterred. After all, numbers alone do not decide battles. The troops were already arranged in a special, extra-wide formation. Their lines stretched far across the riverbank, giving the impression of an army much larger than it truly was. Morale among the soldiers was also high, especially since they were commanded by a seasoned general named Xie Xuan. However, although the Jin army was fearless and disciplined, Xie Xuan knew that he could not depend on brute strength alone to emerge victorious against such a massive force. And so, after days of stalemate—neither side made a move, each waiting for the other's misstep—Xie Xuan devised a strategy. He sent a messenger to the Qin commander, Fu Rong, with a proposal. Xie Xuan requested that the Qin army pull back slightly from the riverbank so that the Jin could cross and face them on equal ground.

When the request was carried to Fu Jian, he immediately gave his blessing; the Qin ruler was confident that such a small move would not make any difference in the outcome of the battle. With his approval, Fu Rong ordered the front lines to step back, clearing space for their enemy to cross. However, in an army of such immense size, where orders had to ripple through countless ranks and languages, misunderstandings spread easily.

When the front lines began to step back, many misunderstood the movement. They believed that retreat had already begun and defeat was in order. Confusion took over the Qin army, followed by panic. Soldiers jostled and stumbled as the line broke its shape. This was the very moment Xie Xuan had been waiting for. Seizing the opportunity, he ordered his troops to advance. Banners were raised and battle cries rose as they charged across the Fei River. The Qin army, so mighty in appearance, collapsed in an instant. Tens of thousands threw down their weapons and fled, while others trampled one another, desperate to retreat.

The defeat destroyed Fu Jian's ambitions. His empire experienced fracture in the years that followed. The Eastern Jin, on the other hand, successfully preserved its existence against all odds.

It is safe to say that war was not a stranger in ancient China. For many centuries, the land had gone through countless episodes of conflict that scarred and shaped the empire. Kingdoms had risen and fallen in waves of chaos, with their borders constantly shifting after each battle. This was especially visible in the age of the Warring States, when it was common to see armies of hundreds of thousands trampling across not only the battlefield but also the countryside. True, peace existed, but it was more of a pause between battles rather than a lasting condition. Out of this chaotic era came the world's most enduring manual of strategy, *The Art of War*. Authored by Sun Tzu, the famed strategist who served the state of Wu, the writings prove useful even to this day.

The Four Greatest Generals of the Late Warring States are highly revered for their contributions to the world of warfare. The first was Lian

Po of Zhao, whose defense strategies at Changping were so effective that even the Qin could not penetrate the city. When he was pulled into intrigue and replaced, Changping was left exposed. His removal opened the way for another great general, Bai Qi of Qin, to make a move. Also known as the "Human Butcher," he was responsible for bringing Qin to multiple glories, including the annihilation of Zhao forces at the Battle of Changping in 260 BCE. Then there was Li Mu, whose careful planning and deception successfully defeated both steppe nomads and Qin armies. He also managed to delay Zhao's fall for years. Last but not least was Wang Jian, whose campaigns crushed Chu (Qin's strongest rival) and gave way for the unification of China.

Yet the fame of Sun Tzu and the Four Great Generals often eclipses others whose loyalty and brilliance were just as vital to their times. Wu Qi, for instance, was one of the overlooked figures whose reforms transformed armies and brought victories. His end, however, was as tragic as his life was extraordinary.

The General Who Valued Merit

Born in the chaotic fifth century BCE, Wu Qi was already used to living a life where peace was far from reach. Since he belonged to a minor noble family, he was given a good education but not a guaranteed position in high office. If he wished to rise through the ranks, Wu Qi must present his worth and talent rather than strictly his inheritance. And so, he began young. The future general filled his early years with studies of military strategies. His earliest career began in the small state of Lu, which was also his mother's homeland. But there he gained only little recognition.

Later on, he entered the service of Wei, at that time considered one of the strongest of the Warring States. Under Marquess Wen, he was given command against the state's greatest rival, Qin. This was the beginning of his glory; Wu Qi demonstrated his brilliance and always struck his enemies with careful calculation.

His talent in warfare shone especially in 389 BCE, when Wei and Qin clashed for dominance in the west. Under his command, the Wei army succeeded in launching a surprise assault on the Qin camp. They also captured the enemy general, forcing the Qin into a hasty retreat. This victory secured Wei's western frontier. Wei faced Qin several more times and, again, Wu Qi distinguished himself. Many more battles were won, further securing Wei's dominance in the Central Plains. By this time, Wu Qi's name had become known far and wide, his victories spoken with the utmost respect.

What placed him apart from all other war generals, however, was his philosophy of leadership. Wu Qi believed victory began with discipline and shared hardship. Hence, despite being rewarded for his achievements, Wu Qi lived just as his men did. He ate coarse rations, slept under the same conditions as his soldiers, and most remarkable of all, even tended to the wounded himself. This undoubtedly won him the respect of common soldiers who would fight alongside him in a heartbeat. But, while Wu Qi was respected by his men, his influence also made him a target in the eyes of the nobility, especially those who felt like their privileges had been stripped away in favor of merit. He eventually fell out of favor with Wei.

Still, Wu Qi refused to stand back despite looming threats. He was later invited to Chu, where he was made chancellor under King Dao. With his new position, Wu Qi continued to build a name. He always preferred merit rather than inheritance or privileges, often giving promotions to capable men regardless of rank. Those deemed incompetent were dismissed.

He enacted reforms that transformed Chu's military and administration and cut corruption, bringing Chu to new heights. The annual salaries of Chu officials were reduced; the saved money flowed into the military so that Chu could train more professional armies. With a stronger force, Wu Qi went on to launch a campaign against the state of Yue. Victory was achieved, which further expanded Chu's borders and restored its influence. With Wu Qi at the helm, Chu grew ever stronger, to the point that it could rival both Qin and Wei.

Unfortunately, history would repeat for Wu Qi. The only difference was that this time, it cost him his life. Wu Qi's policies indeed benefited the state greatly, but his honesty and reforms threatened the aristocrats who had long grown fat off corruption and privilege. The aristocrats knew that to reassert their power, Wu Qi must go. So, when King Dao of Chu passed, they made their move. Archers were hidden at the king's funeral. It was said that Wu Qi immediately spotted the assassins. The *Shiji* narrates that instead of running for cover, the war general leapt to the king's remains. He tried shielding the king's corpse from arrows even as he was struck dead.

The aristocrats succeeded in killing Wu Qi (though they faced punishment for hurting King Dao's corpse) but failed to erase Wu Qi's legacy. The compilation of his military writings, the *Wu Zi*, stands alongside Sun Tzu's *Art of War* as one of the Seven Military Classics of China.

A Scholar Turned General

If Wu Qi's brilliance lay in reshaping the armies of the Warring States, then Ban Chao's genius was in extending Han power far beyond the empire's heartland. His beginnings, however, were rather humble. Ban Chao grew up in a family of scholars. His sister, Ban Zhao, would soon become one of China's most famous female historians. It looked as if the path had been laid for him. Ban Chao was expected to live a quiet life, especially considering he was nothing more than a mere clerk in the Eastern Han court during the first century CE. Instead of riding through battlefields with a sword in hand, he filled his days copying official documents. But, over time, Ban Chao realized that he must pursue another path.

His dreams soon came to reality in 73 CE when the Han launched a major campaign against the Xiongnu. Alongside a military campaign, the Han court also sent smaller envoys on missions into the Western Regions (Tarim Basin) to secure allies and re-establish Han influence over the oasis kingdoms, including the Shanshan, Khotan, and Kashgar. Ancient sources record that Ban Chao was assigned to join this very military expedition as an assistant. This opportunity was possibly given to him because of his family's reputation as respected scholars (especially his father, Ban Biao, and his brother, Ban Gu).

Things changed when the Han envoys arrived at Shanshan. The king of the kingdom appeared hesitant to pledge allegiance to the Han. It also did not help that envoys of Xiongnu had likewise arrived in the region, hoping they could earn the Shanshan king's allegiance. Seeing that the survival of Han influence in Shanshan hung in the balance, Ban Chao chose to make a daring move. With only thirty-six men supporting him, Ban Chao led an attack. Under the cover of the night sky, he and his little band snuck into the Xiongnu camp. The envoys had their guard down, as they did not expect an attack by such a small force of Han envoys. When a blade slashed its first victim, who was sleeping soundly, panic immediately ensued. The Han party cut down its enemy one by one. Ban Chao then presented the severed heads of the envoys to the king of Shanshan. Both stunned and intimidated, the king pledged loyalty to the Han.

From then on, Ban Chao's reputation grew. He moved from oasis to oasis, persuading, intimidating, or defeating local rulers into alliance with the Han. At Khotan and Kashgar, he secured key Silk Road states by playing diplomacy and force in equal measure. Then, in 94 CE, he led campaigns that subdued Kucha and Turfan. By 97 CE, more than fifty states of the Western Regions had acknowledged Han supremacy.

A statue of Ban Chao in Kashgar.[8]

In recognition of his achievements, Ban Chao was appointed protector general of the Western Regions, the highest Han authority in Central Asia. He held the position for more than thirty years, ensuring that the Silk Road remained in Han's control. Ban Chao was also credited with sending an envoy named Gan Ying beyond the borders of China to learn more about the Roman Empire. Gan Ying never reached Rome, but he did set foot on either the eastern coast of the

Mediterranean Sea, the Black Sea, or the Parthian coast of the Persian Gulf. Although he failed to establish direct contact with the Romans, Gan Ying returned with a detailed report that expanded Chinese knowledge of the West.

As for Ban Chao, the deserts and mountains of the west became his home as his duty was tied to the Western Regions. He was relieved of his duty in 102 CE because of his worsening health condition. Ban Chao returned to Luoyang and died of his illness in the same year.

A Reputable General Cut Down By the Emperor

Tan Daoji was a respectable general of the Liu Song dynasty, serving under Emperor Wen. He was active in the first half of the fifth century CE, when the states of Liu Song in the south and Northern Wei in the north were constantly at each other's throats. Though his name is less remembered today, it is hard to dismiss that his campaigns succeeded in preserving the south from northern conquest. The story of his death, however, revealed the perils of loyalty in a world where emperors tend to trust intrigue more than their best generals.

A portrait of Tan Daoji.[9]

When Daoji was born, China was already fragmented. The north had fallen into the hands of non-Han dynasties, while the south was held by the Liu Song. Tan Daoji did not have a slow start to his career. Able to distinguish himself as a soldier with both talent and courage, he grew his reputation rapidly. He was known among his troops for fighting with not only skill but also a sense of fairness and discipline.

His reputation grew even more during the campaigns against the northern states, particularly the Northern Wei. When the north advanced southward, it was Tan Daoji who became the very shield of Liu Song. Of course, this was not the last of his campaigns. Later, Tan Daoji mounted many more counterattacks that left a deep mark on the enemy. This further cemented his reputation and earned him the ultimate devotion of his troops. Even contemporary records praise him as one of the dynasty's most capable commanders. He was described as a man whose leadership allowed the Liu Song to hold its ground against a stronger foe.

But regardless of his enormous contributions to the state, Tan Daoji was not shielded from envious nobles. Like many Chinese generals before him, his growing fame made him a target for intrigue. However, unlike Wu Qi, who faced jealous aristocrats, Tan Daoji was targeted by the emperor himself. Emperor Wen of Liu Song, though a capable ruler, had grown uneasy about Tan Daoji's popularity with the army. Whispers at court also made it worse for the general. Some quietly warned the emperor that the general would soon pose a threat to the dragon throne. Others spoke of the army's devotion to Tan Daoji, suggesting that with such support, the general could usurp the throne by force. In the end, these whispers kept the emperor awake at night. He was certain that Tan Daoji was a man too powerful to be left unchecked.

And so, the general's fate was sealed. The emperor moved against him in 436 CE. Tan Daoji was summoned to court under false pretenses, accused of treason, and arrested. Although the charge was baseless, Tan Daoji was executed. Even two of his most trusted comrades were entangled in the situation and put to death. This brought dire consequences. His loyal soldiers had been left leaderless, and morale collapsed in an instant. Meanwhile, when news of Tan Daoji's death reached Northern Wei, they were said to have rejoiced. Taking advantage of the situation, they advance into Liu Song, wreaking havoc across six provinces. Ancient sources record that Emperor Wen regretted his decision, lamenting that Liu Song would never have faced such destruction if Tan Daoji were alive.

Zhang Heng and Cai Lun

Of course not all of China's great figures left a mark on the battlefield. For every general who defended frontiers or won dynasties, there were men whose genius lay in invention, science, and culture. Take Zhang Heng, for instance. Born in Nanyang (located in present-day Henan Province) during the Eastern Han dynasty, Zhang Heng was known to have displayed his curiosity at an early age. Unlike many of his contemporaries who focused only on Confucian classics, he preferred to dive into the realms of mathematics, astronomy, and mechanics.

As a member of a distinguished family, Zhang Heng unsurprisingly managed to obtain several positions in the court of the Eastern Han. He was even offered a promotion to the role of an imperial secretary. Although this was a high office close to the emperor, Zhang Heng humbly declined the offer. As a man of honesty and principle, he wished to not involve himself in the factional struggles and corruption that often plagued the court. He knew that accepting the position would soon force him into constant conflict with powerful figures. After all, Zhang Heng was far more devoted to astronomy, mathematics, and invention than bureaucratic duties. Instead, he requested to serve as the prefect of Henan. This was a less prominent role, but it allowed him to continue his astronomical studies and inventions.

His greatest achievement came in 132 CE. For years, Zhang Heng had been studying the earth. China was no stranger to earthquakes; thus, he made it his ultimate goal to detect them as they happened, even at great distances. He eventually came up with the device known as the seismoscope. This large bronze vessel was shaped like a barrel. Eight dragons adorned it. Their heads pointed in different directions, and each held a bronze ball in its mouth. Each of these dragons was also accompanied by a bronze toad beneath it. Inside the vessel, Zhang Heng installed a system of levers and pendulums. When an earthquake struck, even one too faint to be felt locally, the mechanism would be activated, causing one dragon to release its bronze ball into the mouth of the waiting toad below. This indicated the direction of the quake. According to historical records, the seismoscope once signaled a quake to the west. Interestingly, messengers arrived at the capital days later, confirming that the device was right: an earthquake had shaken the distant as Zhang Heng's device had indicated.

A replica of Zhang Heng's seismoscope.[10]

Zhang Heng studied not only the earth but also the heavens. He improved the armillary sphere, a device for mapping the stars, and created more accurate calendars by observing celestial movements.

While Zhang Heng measured the earth and heavens, Cai Lun gave us paper. Born in Guiyang (modern-day Hunan), Cai Lun initially entered the palace as a eunuch, possibly in 75 CE, serving Emperor Ming at the end of his reign. He remained a eunuch well until the rise of Emperor He of Han. Details of his early years have been lost to time, but in 105 CE, he made a breakthrough that almost immediately changed the world.

The ancient Egyptians had been writing on papyrus, which was made from the stalks of papyrus reed pressed and dried into sheets. It served well enough along the Nile, but it was fragile, costly to transport, and ill-suited to the needs of a vast empire like Han China. Instead, before Cai Lun presented his idea, the Chinese wrote on bamboo strips, wooden tablets, or in some cases, silk. However, these materials were not suitable in the long run—they were either heavy, cumbersome, or extremely expensive.

A letter written on papyrus, dating to the 3rd century BCE.[11]

Cai Lun, however, introduced a more refined method of creating paper, which he presented to Emperor He. He devised a process of pulping tree bark, hemp, old rags, and fishing nets. The mixture was then strained through a fine screen before being pressed and dried into thin sheets. The result was not only light but also durable and cost effective. This new form of paper undoubtedly revolutionized administration; governments and scholars could record and copy texts way more than before, merchants could keep accounts more efficiently, and ideas could spread more widely than ever.

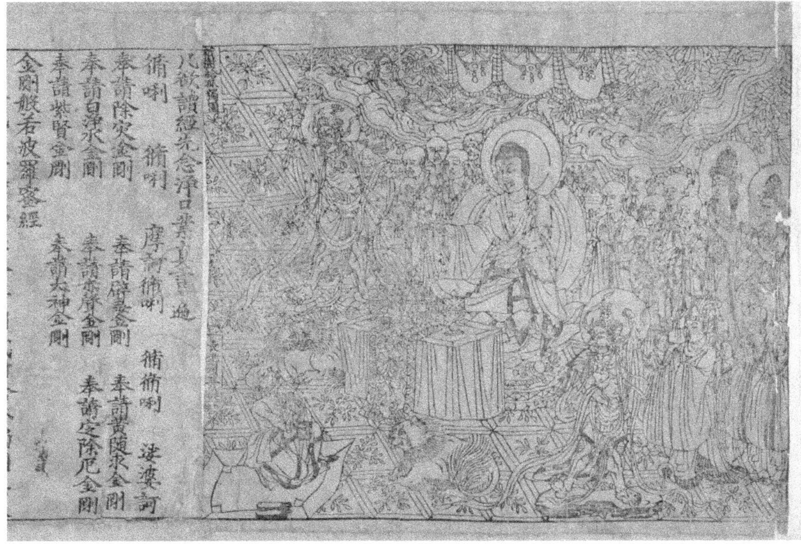

The Diamond Sutra, known as the earliest printed book.[12]

This invention won Cai Lun positions in court and rewards in the form of land. Despite his contributions, Cai Lun was fated to have a rather grim end. When palace politics turned against his faction, he lost imperial favor. Facing disgrace, Cai Lun took his own life by drinking poison in 121 CE.

Chapter 3 – Women Who Defied All Odds

Scanning through the pages of China's early histories, it is easy to notice that most of the stories are crowded with the names of emperors, generals, and ministers. These men were the ones often featured in the annals. Their achievements in grand battles were the ones often recorded with as much detail as possible, along with their edicts, rise, and fall. Names of women, however, are far less visible. When they do appear, it is often in the margins; their names are often accompanied by descriptions like "mother of kings" or "an emperor's favorite" or themes like virtue and caution.

This is not surprising, since from the earliest dynasties, social order was shaped by patriarchal ideals. The ancient Chinese were well acquainted with the doctrine of the Three Obediences. According to Confucius, who taught this doctrine, women were expected to obey their fathers before marriage, their husbands after marriage, and their sons if they were ever widowed. Although this principle was widely accepted in that era, it limited women's independence. Most of the time, a woman was confined to the roles of a daughter, a wife, and a mother. Her virtue was measured by loyalty and modesty within the household rather than personal ambition.

True, there were stark contrasts between the daily lives of female commoners and the elites. Those without prestige typically filled their days weaving, raising children, and managing other household affairs.

Some, especially those in poorer families, also labored in the fields and markets. Among the elites, women did no such thing. More often than not, these mundane chores were assigned to servants while the women enjoy refinement in music, poetry, and calligraphy. However, their talents were meant to polish their husbands' already existing prestige rather than to secure their own. No matter their status, the lives of women in ancient China had boundaries. Legal codes also leaned more toward men, granting them authority over property, marriage, and divorce.

But there were always cracks in the system, allowing a few fortunate women to make a name for themselves—though often, history forgets them. Marriage alliances were one of the ways. Through this small opportunity, women (of noble class, of course) could become imperial consorts or even empresses. They could wield influence, though often precariously, at the side of emperors. In some instances, empress dowagers ruled as regents, at least until the future emperor came of age. There were also times when the imperial concubines altered the balance of power at court.

Meanwhile, outside the palace, there were women who carved their paths as poets and scholars. Some gained authority through religion, particularly Daoism and later Buddhism. This allowed women to step up as priestesses and nuns. And in rare, extraordinary cases, women donned armor, raised banners, and took to the battlefield.

These moments clearly displayed how women were not simply silent figures behind the scenes of history. Despite restrictions, some succeeded in defying the odds, though most of their stories are nearly forgotten. Some were purposely erased, since their narratives did not fit the norm of a patriarchal society. But some of their names appeared in oracle bone inscriptions, and some of their stories survived in fragments of funerary stelae, poems, or the records of reluctant male historians.

One of the findings that sheds more light on women figures of ancient China was made in 1976. Archaeologists were excavating at Yinxu, the ancient Shang capital near Anyang, when they made a surprising discovery. They found a tomb, sealed and undisturbed beneath the layers of earth for over three thousand years. When opened, the tomb revealed an array of precious treasures and artifacts, including over a thousand bronze and jade objects, hundreds of bone implements, and most interesting of all, a variety of weapons.

Fu Hao's burial pit.[18]

In ancient times, not everyone was buried with weapons; they were typically found in tombs belonging to warriors and generals. So, this meant only one thing: the resident of the tomb was known for her martial prowess and involvement in battles and wars. Among other things, they discovered a set of oracle bones. Some of them spoke of a time when six hundred women filled the ranks of the military. Many others had a certain name inscribed on them: Fu Hao.

According to ancient sources, Fu Hao was one of the most extraordinary women in early Chinese history. She lived during the late Shang dynasty, sometime around the thirteenth century BCE. Details of her early life are rather obscure, but evidence suggests that Fu Hao was a high-born princess of a vassal state of the Shang dynasty—possibly a state on the border or the steppe. Given this status, she was bestowed with great education and wealth. When she was only a teenager, Fu Hao found her destiny entangled with that of King Wu Ding of Shang. All those years, the king had been strengthening his position, and one of the ways was to marry a woman from each neighboring tribe. Fu Hao became one of his sixty-four wives, though later she would climb through the ranks, becoming one of the king's three consorts.

However, she lived during a time of war. Seeing that the struggle between Shang and its enemy, the Tufang tribe, had stretched across generations, Fu Hao decided to take bold action. She recommended herself as the general of the Shang army. At first, the king was hesitant, especially when his wife was but a teenage girl. But, since the war had lasted for far too long and his generals seldom returned with news of victory, King Wu Ding reluctantly agreed. The young Fu Hao was sent to the battlefield. Much to everyone's surprise, good news soon arrived at the capital. Their enemy had finally been defeated in a single decisive battle, and Fu Hao was the one who commanded the troops. This was the beginning of her impressive career in the military.

From then on, Fu Hao earned the respect of many, and her achievements continued. Along with her dear husband, Lady Fu Hao succeeded in extending Shang's borders. Campaigns were launched against the neighboring Yi and Qiang. Her most impressive military achievement was when she went against the state of Ba. Backed by two other generals named Xi Li Zhi and Hou Gao, Lady Fu Hao led a force of 13,000 warriors in an ambush against the enemy. This event, inscribed on bones and tortoise shells buried in her tomb, is remembered as one of the earliest large-scale ambushes in the history of China.

Fu Hao did not have her entire attention on military campaigns. She was also a high priestess in charge of the Shang's grand religious ceremonies and sacrificial rituals. Of course, despite having built a name of her own, Fu Hao was also described as a loyal wife to King Wu Ding. The king himself appreciated her so much that stories claim he would wait for his wife's return from war outside the capital city. Once reunited, the two would dismiss their guards so they could spend time together uninterrupted. King Wu Ding also rewarded her greatly for her contributions. The lady was given not only wealth in the form of jewelry, gems, and exquisite silk but also her own land, along with three thousand soldiers for her to command to her liking.

But, unfortunately, Lady Fu Hao did not enjoy a long life. She left the world of the living at the age of thirty-three. Some say she died during childbirth, while others claim she departed due to a lethal wound obtained in a war. King Wu Ding was so saddened by her departure that even in her death, he bestowed a new title upon her. Her posthumous temple name was Mu Xin. The king had two more queens after her death, though these were merely political alliances. Fu Hao, however, was remembered, especially during times of war. The king would invoke her name in official ritualistic ceremonies, seeking her blessings.

Yet unlike most royals, Fu Hao was not buried in the grand royal cemetery. Instead, Wu Ding placed her tomb close to the sacred precinct of Yinxu, perhaps to ensure her spirit remained near the center of ritual life. Because her grave was apart from the usual cluster of royal burials, archaeologists did not find it earlier. Hence, her story remained forgotten until its rediscovery in 1976.

First Female Historian in Chinese History

Ban Zhao was born sometime in 45 CE into a family of scholars. Her father was none other than Ban Biao, a prominent historian during the Han dynasty. Growing up in such a household, Ban Zhao was fortunate to have received a great education and access to valuable books and rare palace manuscripts usually inaccessible for most people. Ban Zhou herself was a lover of knowledge. Ever since she was young, she could often be found surrounded by books and scrolls day and night or involved in debates of history and philosophy with her brothers.

Like most women of her time, Ban Zhao entered married life at an early age—she was only fourteen years old. But not long afterward, her husband died. She never remarried but chose to focus solely on studying literature. Then, another tragedy struck her life, though this one would give her the role that would define her life. Her brother, Ban Gu, was deeply involved in court politics. He was close to Dou Xian, the brother of Empress Dowager Dou. So, when Emperor He launched a coup against Dou Xian in 92 CE, Ban Gu too was dragged down. He was arrested and died in prison the same year. This left the *Book of Han*, initially begun by Ban Biao, incomplete.

The court then requested Ban Zhao, who was already in her forties at that time, to continue the project. She focused especially on the astronomical, ritual, and chronological sections, all of which required scholarly precision. In addition to drafting these sections, Ban Zhao also served as editor for Ban Gu's earlier drafts, ensuring that the document was ready for official presentation. The *Book of Han* was essentially completed around the early 100s CE and later became one of the great official histories of China.

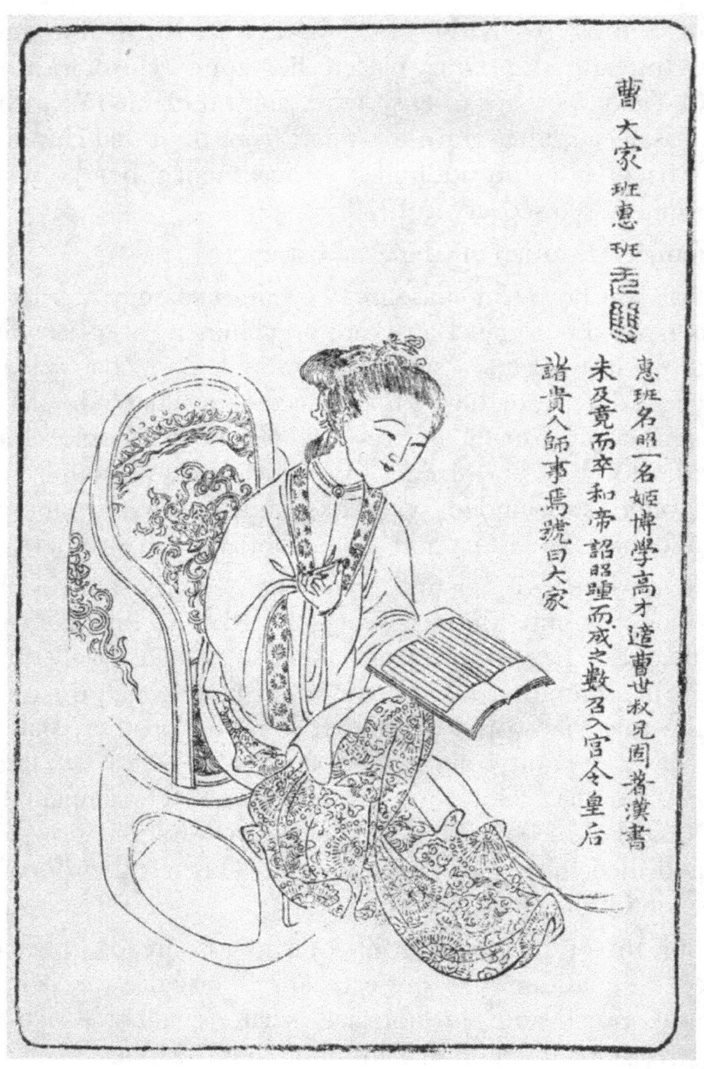

A depiction of Ban Zhao.[14]

Ban Zhao's hands were crucial to the completion of the book, but her accomplishments did not end there. She was also made a tutor, ordered to share her vast knowledge with Empress Deng Sui and the court ladies. She tutored them in literature, history, and etiquette. Because of this, Ban Zhou gained political influence. She was even given the title "Gifted One," and the empress appointed her as a lady-in-waiting. Her wisdom was so precious that the empress consistently sought her advice, even as she became regent for the infant Empress Shang of Han. In gratitude, the empress gave both Ban Zhao's sons appointments as officials.

It was also during this time that Ban Zhao wrote her most famous work, known as *Nü Jie* (Lessons for Women). To modern readers, her work may appear backward or even unreasonable. In her writing, Ban Zhao appeared to have reinforced Confucian ideals of female submission. She emphasized humility, obedience, and advising a woman to yield and be compliant to her husband. This may sound suffocating, especially when we are living in an age that values independence and equality above all. But still, it is hard to dismiss that in the context of the Eastern Han, her work was groundbreaking. She did not instruct a woman to blindly submit to her husband. Instead, she argued that women must receive education, for without it, they would not be able to properly fulfill their roles as wives and mothers. For this reason, some say that her writings were not only extremely influential in her time but also continued to shape ideals of womanhood for centuries. Some scholars even argue that Ban Zhao's work still holds practical applications. Beyond submission, her work also emphasized harmony within households, self-discipline, and the cultivation of moral character—traits that many would agree transcend eras. In this way, her text can be read both as a reflection of Confucian patriarchy and a manual on how women could navigate and survive within its confines.

Ban Zhao died around 116 CE, leaving behind all of her work. Her daughter-in-law, née Ding, collected her works, compiling them into three different volumes known simply as "Collected Works of Ban Zhao." Unfortunately, most of them have been lost to time.

The Princess Who Raised an Army

The Sui dynasty was on the verge of destruction. Famine had swept across the land. Harvests failed, and taxes were as high as the sky itself. The armies had no rest, as they were ordered to march endlessly, building canals, repairing walls, and fighting wars on distant frontiers. Villages were stripped bare; capable men were conscripted, leaving women and children to scrape survival from their barren fields.

Having seen enough chaos, Li Yuan, the commander of the northern frontiers, chose to revolt against Emperor Yang of Sui in 617 CE. He then sent messengers to his daughter, Pingyang, and her husband, General Chai Shao, to join his cause in Taiyuan. However, since they were still in the Sui capital, Chang'an, Chai Shao was worried that it would be impossible for them both to escape without alerting anyone. So, Pingyang advised her husband to depart alone while she figured out another way to quietly leave the city. Chai Shao eventually united with Li Yuan later that year.

Pingyang, on the other hand, went into hiding before she finally left the city in secret. Once out of the city walls, she sought refuge with her relatives across the Yellow River. Knowing that it was unwise for her to remain in hiding while her father and husband instigated a rebellion, Pingyang chose to act. She sold her possessions and distributed her wealth to those who agreed to join the rebellion. Her servants were sent to persuade a few rebel leaders who almost immediately agreed to join arms. She also offered grain to farmers and, according to some sources, even bandits, promising them protection and relief should they choose to join the cause.

With enough numbers, Pingyang began to move. She imposed strict rules of no looting, no harming civilians, and fair trade for supplies. Her discipline distinguished her followers from predatory rebels. As a result, many more flocked to her banner. Her followers, referred to as the Army of the Lady, numbered tens of thousands. One town after another opened its gates, granaries were seized intact, and the roads leading to Chang'an, the Sui capital, were slowly cut away. Couriers no longer dared to ride, and magistrates who resisted were swiftly brought to heel. When her father began marching west, he did so with confidence, knowing that Pingyang had already secured the ground.

Pingyang and her forces provided the support that Li Yuan needed, and he successfully captured Chang'an in November 617 CE. He first installed Emperor Yang's grandson as a puppet ruler. It was only after the emperor's death the following spring that Li Yuan declared himself the new ruler, taking the name Emperor Gaozu. Thus began the era of the Tang dynasty.

As for Pingyang, she lived only for several more years. Her life came to an end in 623 CE when she was only in her twenties. The assumed reason for her death varies, with some claiming she died at childbirth. Others suggest that Pingyang sustained a wound during the rebellion, which later developed into a more serious health implication. Not forgetting her massive contributions to the rebellion, Emperor Gaozu ordered a funeral fit for a war general, complete with music bands. At first, his ministers protested the idea, but the emperor was quick to silence them, exclaiming that the Tang dynasty would have never existed without the help of Pingyang.

The Sorrowful Poet

They were coming for her. Cai Yan, better known by her courtesy name Wenji, was the daughter of Cai Yong, one of the most respected scholars of the late Han dynasty. As a girl born into privilege, all she ever loved was poetry. Cai Yan was married, but not for long; her husband died shortly after their union. She also had no children. Hence, day and night, she would spend her time reading and practicing calligraphy. It was as if she could not live a day without having a brush in her hand. However, no amount of poetry could save her when her town was visited by unwanted guests in 194 CE.

This was a period of turmoil. The Xiongnu had been actively intruding Han territories, causing havoc. One day, these Xiongnu horsemen decided to raid the town where Cai Yan resided. She was kidnapped and taken north, dragged against her will into the untamed steppe and beyond the region she was familiar with. At this point, Cai Yan was certain that her life would soon end. After all, the ancient Chinese had always viewed those from the northern regions as barbarians who preferred the language of violence rather than the ways of civilization.

But the Xiongnu kept her well and alive, albeit as a prisoner. The Xiongnu chief was said to have taken a liking to her, and he eventually claimed her as his wife. From then on, she was treated with the rights due to a consort. She remained with the Xiongnu for twelve long years and even bore the chief two sons. Despite the great treatment she received, Cai Yan never felt at home. There were times when she wept quietly late at night, her heart longing for the life she once had.

Little did she know her time with the Xiongnu was almost over. Back in China, the warlord Cao Cao had already risen to power. Having consolidated the fractured Han empire, he soon moved to rescue Cai Yan. The reason behind his decision is never confirmed, but scholars suggest that he knew her father, Cai Yong. To honor the family, he chose to bring Cai Yan back. She was also the only one left of her clan.

Cao Cao negotiated with the Xiongnu chieftain. After he paid a large sum, Cai Yan's release was finally secured. Although she could finally return, just as she had always wished every night, Cai Yan departed with a heavy heart. According to Xiongnu tradition, children must remain with their father. Therefore, Cai Yan was forced to leave her sons behind.

A drawing of Cai Yan drafting her poetry.[15]

Upon returning to the land she once called home, Cai Yan was married to a government official named Dong Si. She had regained her freedom, yet the memory of her life far from the borders never left her. And so, she picked up a brush and began pouring out her thoughts and feelings. She composed works that captured both her grief and resilience. Known as the "Eighteen Songs of a Nomad Flute," her writings were remembered especially for their sorrowful tones. The verses spoke of life on the frontier, the endless winds of the steppe, the ache of separation, and the loneliness of a woman caught between two worlds.

Her story is unusual not only for its tragedy but also for its survival. While countless women endured captivity and loss during the fall of the Han, Cai Yan's voice is one of the few that still reaches us, carried in poems attributed to her and in the stories retold by later historians.

The Female Minister

You may have heard of Wu Zetian. She was known to be the only woman in ancient China to ever sit on the throne, ruling in her own right. Her name is often included in books as a symbol of female power in a world that rarely allowed it. Not so many, however, remember the name Shangguan Wan'er, whose influence grew at the same time Wu Zetian was carving her destiny.

In contrast to Cai Yan, whose story began with peace, Wan'er's began in blood. Her grandfather, Shangguan Yi, was once a high-ranking minister. Things took a darker turn, however, when he fell out of favor with the empress. It is said that Shangguan Yi grew so discontent with the empress's controlling behavior that he proposed to Emperor Gaozong that the empress be deposed. Empress Wu eventually learned this and immediately planned for his removal. She accused the minister of treason, resulting in the execution of Shangguan Yi and much of his family. Wan'er, who was only a child at that time, was spared but was condemned to palace servitude.

But Wan'er had a gift for words. She could compose elegant poetry and draft documents with both precision and grace. Her talent soon attracted the attention of those in the palace, including Wu Zetian herself. Recognizing her brilliance, the empress chose to bury the hatchet and took Wan'er into her inner court. From then on, her influence soared. Wan'er became Wu Zetian's secretary and eventually her voice. Her words mattered most, second only to the empress. From crafting verses, Shangguan Wan'er's responsibilities grew to include polishing proclamations, drafting imperial edicts, and advising the empress on state matters.

Of course, she was more than just a mere scribe. Wan'er knew that relationships with the other court officials were important if she were to survive the world of politics. Consequently, she never shied away from mingling with scholars and officials, often hosting gatherings where poetry and politics were discussed. Some say she could match wits with even the empire's greatest minds, and her literary salons gave her influence beyond the written page. Chroniclers also note that when disputes arose, many waited to see how Shangguan Wan'er would phrase the matter, for her words could tip the balance of interpretation. Her role in the court was so important that contemporaries refer to her as the "female prime minister." It is safe to say that only a few women in

Chinese history ever wielded such recognized, practical authority without sitting on the throne.

Her influence did not disappear even after Wu Zetian died in 705 CE. When Emperor Zhongzong rose to the throne, Wan'er became one of his concubines. Aware of her experience and abilities, he entrusted Wan'er with matters of the state, especially in drafting edicts. She also became the confidant of the emperor's wife, Empress Wei. This, however, was the beginning of her fall.

Empress Wei dreamed of following the footsteps of Wu Zetian. Thus, when Emperor Zhongzong died in 710 CE, she was quick to make a move. The empress persuaded Wan'er to assist her: she was tasked with drafting a fake pre-dated will detailing the late emperor's wish to pass the throne to his son and the regency to the empress. But, a coup soon erupted, led by a rival to the throne, Li Longji (the son of Emperor Taizong), who allied with his aunt, Princess Taiping. Li Longji killed Empress Wei, along with her clan members. Li Longji and his men then made their way to the pavilion where Shangguan Wan'er lived. Sources described how Wan'er stepped out of the pavilion to greet Li Longji. She hoped to be spared from the bloodshed, but Li Longji had already made up his mind. In the end, Shangguan Wan'er was beheaded.

Chapter 4 – Kill or Be Killed

The forces of Qin under King Zheng were unstoppable. By the late third century BCE, they had already emerged victorious over two rivals: Han, the weakest of the seven states, and Zhao, the more formidable one. With the fall of these two states, the Qin looked no further to secure yet another victory. This time around, they turned their gaze to Yan, a northeastern kingdom of mountains and river valleys.

Of course, Qin's advances toward the state were not a secret. King Xi of Yan himself knew that his state did not stand a chance against the powerful Qin. Therefore, to preserve peace, he offered his son, Crown Prince Dan, as a diplomatic hostage to Qin. Such hostage arrangements were common, especially in the ancient world. (Rome would later take sons of conquered kings to ensure loyalty, just as the Greeks once held prominent figures as hostages to guarantee alliances.)

Diplomatic hostages like Prince Dan were not supposed to be treated like any other lowly hostages put in shackles following a battle. However, records suggest that, despite starting off well, King Zheng eventually began treating the crown prince poorly. This filled Prince Dan with resentment. Humiliated that he was seen as a pawn rather than a prince, he began to plan an attempt many deemed impossible: assassinate King Zheng and save the state of Yan from the upcoming grasp of Qin.

Following his return to Yan, Prince Dan wasted no time in planning his mission. In hopes of securing a higher chance of succeeding, he began searching for a man of rare courage. As if the heavenly gods were on his side, the prince found the individual through his friend, Tian Guang.

"I may have the exact man who could defy the odds and ensure the success of your mission," Tian Guang likely said to Prince Dan.

The man was known as Jing Ke. Born in the minor state of Wey, he was far more than just an ordinary retainer. Jing Ke was not only given good education in his younger years but also well versed in martial arts; he was especially skilled in swordsmanship. Jing Ke was said to have remained in his homeland of Wey until the state was annexed by Qin in 239 BCE. From then on he fled, eventually arriving in Yan, where his disdain for Qin aligned with that of the crown prince.

Having found someone to carry out the mission, Prince Dan began concocting the assassination. The plan was to strike the king of Qin with a poisoned dagger. Procuring the sharpest dagger available and lining it with poison was a walk in the park. Approaching the king with the weapon, however, required a smart scheme. Jing Ke proposed to mask the assassination with an audience of surrender. He planned to get the king's attention by offering him two tokens of loyalty: the severed head of the man who betrayed Qin and a map of Dukang, the first region of Yan that Qin desired.

The first token required a sacrifice. The story goes that Jing Ke himself traveled to meet the traitor. Known as Fan Yuqi (identified in some accounts as Huan Yi), he was once a loyal Qin general. He had fallen out of favor with the king of Qin, who was said to have placed a bounty of one thousand gold pieces on his head. Jing Ke knew that Fan Yuqi harbored resentment and would not hesitate to exact revenge on King Zheng. So, when the plan for assassinating the king was laid before him, the former Qin general immediately agreed to get his hands dirty, although he would not be able to witness the downfall of the king. He took his own life so that his severed head could be offered as a prize to King Zheng.

With the first gift successfully in his hands, Jing Ke then prepared the second one. He rolled the silk map of Dukang with care. Within it concealed the poisoned dagger, which he would use to end the life of the merciless king.

Jing Ke was not to travel alone. Prince Dan had already assigned a youth named Qin Wuyang to assist Jing Ke in his mission. Qin Wuyang was not a nobody; he was infamously known for having committed murder at the young age of thirteen. While Jing Ke bore the map, Qin Wuyang carried the head of Fan Yuqi.

The two entered the capital of Qin, Xianyang, in 227 BCE. The court officials marveled at the grisly display of Fan Yuqi's severed head. They were confident that Jing Ke, who had arrived under the guise of an ambassador of Yan, meant no harm and was only pleading for the king's mercy. The next move was to present the map to the king.

But tension made its first appearance in the episode when Qin Wuyang found himself frozen. He faltered as he approached the throne, completely struck by fear in the presence of the Son of Heaven. Jing Ke was quick to cover the situation. He apologized for his companion's sudden paralysis, excusing it as the common reaction of a youth awed by the splendor of the royal court. Still, the guards intervened. They barred Qin Wuyang from taking a step further and ordered Jing Ke to proceed alone.

As if he had practiced the scene multiple times, Jing Ke approached King Zheng and presented the map. The king unrolled the scroll while the courtiers leaned forward to get a clearer view. The very moment the dagger was revealed, Jing Ke snatched it without hesitation. He seized the king's sleeve and thrust in the poisoned dagger. But King Zheng managed to dodge the strike, ripping his sleeve in the process.

A mural depicting the assassination attempt.[16]

The king desperately tried to unsheathe the long ceremonial sword that hung at his side, but it proved too cumbersome to draw while running. At this point, it looked as if his fate had been sealed. No minister near him was armed since it was customary for them to leave their weapons outside during royal ceremonies, and the guards were stationed outside the hall. Suddenly, a physician named Xia Wuju intervened. He threw his medicine bag at Jing Ke, who stumbled for a few seconds. This was enough time for the king to gain more distance from his assassin and finally unsheathe his sword.

Now armed, King Zheng struck at Jing Ke, running his blade across the assassin's thigh. Jing Ke, refusing to surrender that easily despite bleeding heavily, hurled the dagger toward the king. But, instead of hitting King Zheng, the dagger accidentally landed on a pillar. Seizing the opportunity, the king drove his long ceremonial sword into Jing Ke again and again, stabbing him a total of eight times.

Jing Ke collapsed, but using the last of his strength, he sat upright with his legs splayed. This was a posture considered gravely rude. He then threw curses at the king. Guards, having finally stormed into the chamber, finished him off. Qin Wuyang was said to have attempted to flee the palace grounds but was unfortunately cut down by the royal guards.

Silence soon filled the air. Only the ragged breath of the king could be heard. He slowly returned to his throne and was said to have sat there motionless while still clutching his bloodied sword. When he finally caught his breath, King Zheng turned to the physician Xia Wuju and thanked him for his desperate act that slowed Jing Ke's movement.

The state of Yan would face Qin's wrath. Prince Dan sent his army to put up a fight, yet all was already written: Yan must fall under Qin. King Xi of Yan again tried to appease the King of Qin by ordering the death of his own son. Yet, this did not accomplish anything. His state was annexed and destroyed.

With Yan subdued, the rest of China soon followed. By 221 BCE, King Zheng of Qin succeeded in uniting the lands. He rose as Qin Shi Huang, the first emperor of unified China. It was the start of a new age.

The Burning of Books and Burying of Scholars under Qin Shi Huang

Of course, wars and battles were not the only things the emperor had to deal with to ensure the stability of his newly founded empire. He also had to reshape the thoughts of his people.

The emperor's chosen ideology was Legalism, which demanded strict laws, severe punishments, and absolute obedience. But this doctrine was not welcomed by all, especially Confucian scholars. For generations, they served as moral critics of kings and advisors in courtly ethics. Their teachings spoke of the virtue of rulers, the Mandate of Heaven, and of course, the importance of tradition. Basically, Confucianism suggested that a ruler's legitimacy depended upon benevolence and moral example, an idea that conflicted with the Legalist doctrine that Qin Shi Huang greatly championed.

The clash came to a head in 213 BCE. Scholars had been increasingly and openly criticizing imperial policies. When Qin Shi Huang finally had enough, the king ordered what became known as the "burning of books." Texts that did not serve the regime's practical purposes were thrown into the flames. These texts—particularly the classics of poetry, history, and Confucian ritual—included the Book of Documents, the Book of Songs, and histories of rival states. The government only saved works on medicine, agriculture, and divination.

This erasure of knowledge and memory did not stop there. The following year, the emperor unleashed yet another violent order. According to the *Shiji*, the emperor proclaimed hundreds of scholars guilty for sowing discord just because they clung to the old ways. They were ordered to be buried alive. But this gruesome event has always been a matter of dispute. Some scholars suggest it may not have occurred as described, while others agree that it happened but might have been a smaller, more targeted event or perhaps a misinterpretation of other punishments.

The Xuanwu Gate Incident

The Xuanwu Gate Incident is a story of brotherly rivalry. It all began when Emperor Gaozu of the Tang dynasty named his eldest son, Li Jiancheng as crown prince. This, of course, did not sit well with a few others in the empire. Some whispered that despite being the first born, it was not Li Jiancheng who should succeed Gaozu, but the younger Li Shimin. This was not surprising since Li Shimin had already proven himself on the battlefield, especially when the Tang dynasty was still struggling to climb its way to supremacy. Li Shimin had led his forces against multiple formidable adversaries; he defeated the warlord Dou Jiande, who controlled much of Hebei, and crushed Wang Shichong, who once dared to declare himself emperor in Luoyang. Through these major victories, Li Shimin's influence grew tremendously. Soldiers hailed him as a respected commander, and scholars viewed him as the right fit for the throne.

Li Jiancheng, on the other hand, was not bestowed with the same opportunities as his younger brother. He was stationed along the northern frontier, where he was responsible for protecting the empire from the Tujue (powerful Turkic nomads of the steppe). Although this was indeed an important assignment, his position far from Chang'an (the capital of the Tang dynasty) made it difficult for the crown prince to outshine Li Shimin.

It also did not help when Emperor Gaozu himself acknowledged Li Shimin's growing influence. Perhaps seeing the potential in his son, the emperor gave him control over the civil and military administration of the eastern plain, based in Luoyang (the old imperial capital). This allowed Li Shimin to establish a second court of his own, which he filled with fifty handpicked civil and military officials. The prince even established the College of Literary Studies and appointed eighteen scholars who also constantly advised him on matters of state. This stirred discontent within Li Jiancheng. He was afraid that his brother would soon be ambitious enough to go for the throne. He shared this view with his other younger brother, Li Yuanji.

By the early 620s, the relationship between the brothers had turned extremely sour; it eventually hardened into suspicion and venom. At the beginning of their rivalry, it was hard to predict the ending. Li Jiancheng had the title, chosen by the emperor himself, and the strong support of Li Yuanji. On the other side of the ring, Li Shimin had influence, fame, and loyal allies from the capital.

They did not fight each other with swords on the battlefield. Some said Li Jiancheng and Li Yuanji once tried to slip poison into Li Shimin's cup. Whether this was true or just a rumor remains unconfirmed. What is certain, however, is that the rivalry between the brothers also dragged others down. There was a time when Li Jiancheng and Li Yuanji pointed their fingers to Li Shimin's most trusted advisors, Fan Xuanling and Du Ruhui. The princes lobbied against them, resulting in their dismissal from service. They also once attempted an assassination on Li Shimin's most loyal general, Yuchi Jingde. When this failed, the two slandered Yuchi Jingde at court, which would certainly have cost his life if Li Shimin himself had not intervened in the matter.

Li Shimin was not always a favorite among the officials behind the walls of Chang'an, especially when he was frequently away on campaigns. This created an opportunity for Li Jiancheng and Li Yuanji to elevate their influence. They stayed close to the emperor and enjoyed the support of Gaozu's favored consorts.

But Li Shimin was a clever prince. He knew that to defeat those who played dirty, he must not remain silent. It was better to strike than to be struck. He chose to end everything once and for all at Xuanwu Gate, the northern entrance to the imperial palace. It was heavily guarded and narrow, making it feasible for Li Shimin to trap his brothers. Most importantly, the prince also had an ally stationed there.

"I need your loyalty, Chang He," Li Shimin may have said to his ally.

Years prior, Chang He served under the prince as an officer. In 624 CE, he was reassigned to command the troops at the Xuanwu Gate. Li Shimin bribed his ally and gave a simple order: when the moment came, Chang He and his soldiers were to obey Li Shimin rather than the crown prince.

Next was to think of a way to lure his brothers to the gate. This was when Li Shimin played his boldest card. He submitted a memorial to Emperor Gaozu, accusing his two brothers of illicit affairs with several of the emperor's consorts. It is plausible that many found the claim scandalous and hard to believe. Yet, Gaozu could not ignore it, especially coming from his son, who had given the empire many victories. Therefore, he summoned Li Shimin for an audience the following morning.

News of the accusation spread, eventually reaching the ears of one of the emperor's consorts, Zhang. With haste, the consort sent words to Li Jiancheng, informing the crown prince of the accusations made by his ambitious younger brother. With forces ready, Li Jiancheng and his loyal brother, Li Yuanji, rode toward the palace, hoping they could consult the emperor personally.

Little did the brothers know they were heading directly into a trap. They entered Xuanwu Gate and, almost immediately, could feel a sense of heavy tension. Li Shimin, knowing that his brothers were about to turn back, spurred his horse forward.

"Stay, my brothers!" Li Shimin said.

Li Yuanji reacted by drawing his bow, hoping he could cut down his brother before the ambush could take place. Yet, his hands betrayed him. The bowstring slipped, and he failed to take the shot. Seizing the chance, Li Shimin immediately shot an arrow, which went through the crown prince. Li Jiancheng fell off his horse, lifeless.

Panic undoubtedly ensued afterward. Li Yuanji escaped the scene with Yuchi Jingde and seventy of his horsemen pursuing him. Arrows were let loose. and one struck true. Li Yuanji fell from his horse, but this was not yet the end of the prince. Li Shimin, determined to eliminate his brother, gave chase. However, as he entered the woods, his horse went out of control. Its reins snagged on the branches, and Li Shimin was thrown to the ground. Seeing a chance to survive, Li Yuanji scrambled to his brother's side. Seizing Li Shimin's own bow, he pressed the weapon against his brother's throat. Fortunately for Li Shimin, his loyal general, Yuchi Jingde, was on his way.

Hearing the distant sounds of hooves, Li Yuanji quickly moved away from his brother. Desperate, the prince fled on foot toward Wude Hall, his residence within the eastern section of the palace. However, death was ready for him. Yuchi Jingde eventually caught up with Li Yuanji before the prince could reach the gates. Like Li Jiancheng, an arrow found a target in Li Yuanji. His flesh was pierced, and he laid dead.

The heads of both princes were then severed and carried back to Xuanwu Gate, where a fight was taking place between the forces of Li Jiancheng and Li Shimin (led by Chang He). Upon witnessing the severed heads of the princes, the fight immediately stopped.

The emperor, on the other hand, was completely unaware of the bloodshed. According to the *Jiu Tangshu* (Old Book of Tang, a tenth-century official history of the dynasty) and the *Zizhi Tongjian* (Comprehensive Mirror to Aid in Government, an eleventh-century chronicle by Sima Guang), Emperor Gaozu was sailing leisurely on a lake within the palace city when the coup erupted. Li Shimin, knowing that it was wise to report the event to the emperor, sent Yuchi Jingde to deliver the news. Startled, the emperor threw questions to Yuchi Jingde; he demanded to know the reason behind the chaos and the names of those who dared to disturb the peace. Yuchi Jingde calmly reported the outcome of the incident. He explained that the deaths of the two princes were necessary for the preservation of order and claimed that the two brothers were indeed a disturbance of peace.

Sources suggest that although he accepted the explanation, Emperor Gaozu was puzzled and uncertain of what should be done. Hence, he turned to his officials. Not long after, two courtiers stepped forward to voice their opinion. They exonerated Li Shimin completely, praising his past victories. They claimed that killings of Li Jiancheng and Li Yuanji were nothing more than a righteous punishment. From this point on, it was clear that the court supported Li Shimin as the new crown prince.

Despite being a step closer to the throne, Li Shimin refused to lay low. Loyalists of Li Jiancheng and Li Yuanji still existed, scattered through the capital. And so, Li Shimin relied once more on Yuchi Jingde, who successfully urged Gaozu to issue an imperial edict ordering all resistance to cease and commanding the remaining troops to submit to the victorious prince.

Three days later, the emperor officially announced Li Shimin as the new heir apparent. Li Shimin enjoyed this new title for only a few weeks. Gaozu soon abdicated the throne, giving way for Li Shimin to rise as Emperor Taizong of Tang.

The Lü Clan Purge

In 195 BCE, Emperor Gaozu of Han (not to be confused with the later Gaozu of Tang) lay on his deathbed. He was suffering from a wound obtained during one of his military campaigns. Of course, whenever a ruler came close to his demise, the same question lingered: who would soon sit on the throne?

The most obvious answer to this question was the crown prince, Liu Ying, the son of the emperor with his wife, Lü Zhi. However, conflict soon came when Gaozu displayed affection for Lady Qi, who eventually became known as his most favored concubine. Together, they had a son named Liu Ruyi. Rumors had been going around claiming that the emperor himself desired to see Liu Ruyi named heir in place of his son with Lü Zhi. In Gaozu's eyes, Liu Ruyi was more spirited and capable, while Crown Prince Liu Ying was considered gentle, perhaps too meek for the throne.

This favoritism undoubtedly planted the seed of bitterness, which over time would grow into violence. Lü Zhi not only hated Lady Qi for securing the emperor's affection, but she also resented her for giving birth to a son who posed a threat to Liu Ying's future. Still, she concealed her resentment while Gaozu lived. But when the emperor finally let out his final breath, the empress knew it was high time to show her true colors.

Gaozu was succeeded by Liu Ying, who ruled as Emperor Hui of Han. His mother became empress dowager. The new emperor was kind-hearted but, at the same time, a tad pliable. In just a short time, he fell into his mother's hands. Empress Dowager Lü Zhi wasted no time in securing her position—after all, this was the time she had long been waiting for. She sidelined ministers she distrusted and elevated her own relatives to key posts. Although Emperor Hui was positioned on top of the hierarchy, behind the scenes, it was his mother who moved the chess pieces.

Of course, Lady Qi would soon face the wrath of the empress dowager. With her husband gone, the empress was free to exact her revenge. She had Lady Qi stripped of favor and thrown into a dungeon. This, however, was not the worst of her punishment for being the object of the former emperor's affection. Lady Qi was also heavily mutilated. First, Lü Zhi had the poor concubine's hair shaved clean. Then, she moved to features that may have once been the favorites of Emperor Gaozu. Lady Qi's eyes were gouged and her ears severed. She was also forced to drink a type of potion that rendered her mute. As if this wasn't enough, the empress dowager also had the concubine's limbs chopped off before throwing her into a latrine and later a pigsty. It took a while before Lady Qi died. To ensure she remained alive to taste the agonizing torture, Lü Zhi force-fed her.

It was said that the empress dowager presented the terrifying state of the concubine to her son. Emperor Hui was left horrified. Legend has it that the sight of Lady Qi scarred him deeply and broke his spirit to the point that he chose wine drinking rather than active governance. His withdrawal from government opened the door for his mother to wield power unchallenged.

Emperor Hui died at the young age of twenty-two in 188 BCE. The crown was then passed to his young son, who was enthroned as Emperor Qianshao of Han. Like his late father, Qianshao was also reduced to the status of a figurehead. It was still Empress Dowager Lü Zhi who dictated the workings of the empire.

Some would say that, on one hand, she presided over an era of relative stability. Taxes remained moderate, and the empire did not face the same crushing levies that had characterized the Qin. The harshness of Legalist rule was softened, and agriculture thrived. Yet for all these policies, discontent simmered in court, especially when it was clear that Lü Zhi gave her full attention to staffing the government with her own kin. Years prior, Emperor Gaozu—with Lü Zhi's advice—had issued a ruling that only members of the imperial Liu clan could obtain high offices. The decree was intended to secure the dynasty's legitimacy by preventing the rise of rival houses. But, ironically, it was Lü Zhi herself who maneuvered to undo this.

She elevated her relatives to high offices. Brothers, nephews, and cousins of the Lü clan were granted the titles of kings and marquises, privileges reserved for the emperor's bloodline. Entire fiefdoms were carved out for her family, often at the expense of the Liu clan's own power. Zhe Lü's careful appointments ensured that the most critical posts were dominated by her kin. Eventually, it was as if a parallel dynasty of Lü was being established within the Han itself.

But few dared to challenge her openly. Things only changed in 180 CE, when the power-hungry empress died. With the only shield protecting the Lü clan off the surface of the earth, resentment that had smoldered for years erupted. The purge began almost immediately. It was orchestrated by senior ministers who had once served Emperor Gaozu and remained loyal to the Liu imperial line. With the support of imperial princes, they struck at the Lü clan before it could rally.

It was merciless. Lü family members were seized from their posts, stripped of their titles, and executed. Some were forced to take their own lives, while others were slaughtered outright. Entire households, including women and children, regardless of their age, were obliterated to prevent any future threat. Within days, the once-dominant Lü clan was reduced to corpses and ashes. It is safe to say that they were erased from political life.

With the clan extinguished, the ministers restored the balance of power to the Liu family. The throne was eventually passed to benevolent Emperor Wen, a distant son of Gaozu, whose reign welcomed a new era of prosperity.

Chapter 5 – Legends That May Have Some Truth in Them

The rivers refused to rest. Seasons passed, yet the waters swelled beyond their banks, drowning fields, homes, and sweeping away entire villages. What should have been fertile plains became dangerous lakes, forcing families to cling to whatever patches of dry earth remained. In contrast to the ancient Egyptians, who viewed the predictable inundation of the Nile as a blessing from their gods, the Chinese faced a different kind of deluge. While the Nile flooding revitalized the many crops of Egypt, in China, the floods looked as if they were threatening to undo a civilization. They came like an uninvited storm—chaotic and destructive.

The misery of his people was getting louder. The ruling emperor at that time, Emperor Yao (one of the legendary sage-kings) began to desperately look for a way to tame the disaster. His attention was eventually brought to a man named Gun. He summoned the man to his palace and entrusted him with the important task of stopping the flood. It was indeed a tough mission; going against mother nature always ended with more destruction. But still, Gun was determined. He came up with a rather bold strategy that included building massive dikes to confine the waters. He envisioned barriers so strong and high that the rivers would be forced back into their channels, subdued by the will of man.

Of course, realizing such a project would take years, and it demanded both labor and sacrifice from countless communities. But it must be done. So, the emperor supplied Gun with dozens of people from all over the land, tasked with heaping earth and stone into towering walls. Villagers who had once farmed their fields now carried baskets of soil on their backs, marching in long lines to raise defenses against the waters. They toiled for months with little rest. At last, walls of earth rose where rivers had once surged freely. The people rejoiced, convinced that the days of turmoil had finally come to an end. They watched as the floodwaters gathered behind the dykes they had successfully built. But over time, the people grew worried once more, especially when it was clear that the rivers remained restless.

Each day, the rivers pressed harder against the walls, heightening the anxiety of the people. When the embankments finally gave way, the destruction that followed was undoubtedly catastrophic. In just moments, the fields drowned completely, and villages were carried away. Many lives were lost. All those years of labor went to waste, for the flood refused to be tamed. Gun had failed.

Interestingly, later tradition added a more mythical reason for his failure. The story goes that Gun had wronged the gods by stealing a magical substance known as *xi rang*. With the celestial self-expanding soil in his possession, Gun placed it upon the earth, causing it to grow endlessly into towering dikes; whenever the water rose, so did the dike. However, his theft did not go unnoticed. Angered, the gods cursed his construction.

Whether the failure was a direct result of the gods' wrath or simply caused by human miscalculation, Gun's effort ended in total disaster, to the point that he, too, met a rather grim end. Some recalled Gun being executed under the order of the new ruler, Emperor Shun, while others claimed he committed suicide by leaping into an abyss. There were also those who talked about Gun being cursed and turned into an animal.

While Gun's demise and failure is often shrouded in myth, many agreed that before he died, Gun passed the responsibility of building the dykes to his son named Yu. At first, many doubted Yu could do any better. They believed that they were doomed to the flood and none could change that. Emperor Shun, however, saw something in Yu that others overlooked. He sensed a quiet determination in him. He knew that Yu was the key to freeing his people from these years of agony. This came to be true because Yu understood the flood differently. While Gun had sought to conquer the waters with force, Yu believed that mastery would come only through respect.

So, he did not begin his task by building walls that could reach the heavens. Instead, he began with observation. For a few years, he traveled across the land, hoping he could trace the restless Yellow River from its upper reaches in the west to its swollen belly in the Central Plains. He studied the valleys, the mountains, the floodplains, and the natural courses through which the waters longed to run. Where Gun had seen only an enemy to be resisted, Yu saw a partner to be guided.

His solution was to channel rather than block. Again, thousands of laborers were gathered to work on the project. However, instead of relying on dykes, Yu planned to cut trenches and open canals. This way, he could carve new pathways through the earth. Without wasting any more precious time, the workers dug great channels to link the swollen rivers to lakes and marshes that could bear the excess. In some places, Gu widened the existing streams. In others, he ordered that new courses be carved entirely, allowing the water to escape toward the distant sea. The plan seemed to be going so well that villagers who had once fled the waters joined in the effort. In time, the floods that once drowned the fields and took the lives of many began to flow and spread more evenly.

Of course, a lot of time was spent to ensure the success of the project. Even Yu partook in the project with his own hands rather than merely standing and giving out orders. According to legend, Yu labored for thirteen years without rest. He dragged himself across provinces and mountain ranges, equipped only with a rough mat to sleep on under the dark night sky. He was so dedicated to saving his people that did not even meet his family. It is said that he passed by his home three times during the mission. Each time, his family, particularly his son, called for him to stop by and rest. Yet, he continued walking, refusing to even turn to his family for a smile. In his mind, to pause, even for a moment of comfort, was to neglect the burden of his duty. True, the story may be exaggerated, but the point is clear: Yu was a man who placed the well-being of his people above all else.

His effort proved fruitful. Fields and crops that were once consumed by the relentless flood were restored to farmers. Roads and villages that were destroyed were rebuilt, allowing the people to thrive once more. Indeed, the Yellow River was still unpredictable, but it was at least manageable.

Emperor Shun was impressed by Yu's strategy and effort, to the point that he raised him to the highest honors. Yu continued to serve the court, displaying his bright mind and talent. He was eventually appointed to command the imperial armies, in charge of defending the southern frontiers from the Sanmiao people. This unruly tribe had been a thorn to the kingdom, especially when it had taken advantage of the floods to raid vulnerable villages.

It is not surprising to learn that Yu led his men against the enemy with the same perseverance he had shown against the waters. Not once did he ever strike before thinking; he was said to be an excellent commander who often studied the land and turned it to his advantage. The campaign against the Sanmiao was undoubtedly fierce, but Yu emerged victorious, driving them away from the borders. Peace was restored to the kingdom, and the people praised him for protecting them not only from nature but also from human enemies.

Then, when it was high time for the emperor to choose a successor, Yu made it to the top of the list. This was a time when rulers were chosen by merit rather than bloodline. Emperor Shun himself was not the son of the previous emperor, Yao. But his capabilities and achievements made him visible to his predecessor, and when the time came, he was the one to wear the crown. Now, Emperor Shun did the same. He elevated Yu above others, including his own bloodline, because of his great deeds, achievements, and character.

Yu, the Great

Possible location of the Xia dynasty and the nine provinces established by Yu.[17]

According to tradition, Yu rose to the throne sometime in 2070 BCE. He was an active ruler, traveling constantly across his kingdom and holding audiences with his ministers to discuss matters of the land and things that troubled his subjects. It is safe to say that his reign marked a turning point. He was also responsible for dividing the kingdom into nine provinces. Tribute systems were introduced, and each province was expected to pay in bronze. This bronze was then forged into the Nine Tripod Cauldrons, which are among the most famous legendary artifacts in Chinese tradition. Among Yu's first acts after receiving the Mandate of Heaven, these cauldrons were meant to show the unification of the different regions under Yu's rule. The cauldrons were then passed down as symbols of legitimacy from dynasty to dynasty, much like the crown jewels in later European monarchies. Unfortunately, the Nine Tripod Cauldrons disappeared during the late Zhou. Some said they sank deep into the Si River, never to be recovered again.

Despite being a capable ruler, Yu was but a mortal man; he too could not escape death. As the years of his reign waned, Yu knew it was time to choose a successor. The story goes that he at first intended to pass the throne to his trusted minister. However, the people favored his son, Qi, who as a boy had lived through the troubling time of the flood. The boy endured his father's absence without lamenting or complaining about it. This led the people to predict that the boy possessed the same endurance and strength of character that marked his father.

However, Yu hesitated since he did not want to put the heavy weight of rule onto his son's shoulders. Yet, the people refused to forget their view. They remembered Qi as the one who had suffered his father's sacrifice, and they revered him as the natural heir. Eventually, after convening with his officials, who also threw their support behind Qi, Yu relented. He named his son as his successor, thus breaking the ancient tradition of merit-based succession. This marked the beginning of the Xia dynasty. From ruler to son, from father to heir, authority would now pass along bloodlines.

Perhaps mirroring his father, Qi was a capable ruler. However, his son, Tai Kang, did not live up to the weight of that legacy. When the throne was passed to him, Tai Kang ruled with a steady hand at first, but he eventually chose indulgence rather than governance. His negligence soared until his land began to suffer. This, however, was not the end of the Xia dynasty. It continued to witness a set of successors, many of whom were said to have been highly skilled.

The sixth ruler was named Shao Kang, who, according to tradition, was thought to be the restorer of the kingdom. Before he rose, ancient China was fraught with peril. His own father was a victim of civil strife. When his father died, Shao Kang lived in obscurity until he grew strong enough to return and reclaim his inheritance. To his people, he was a hero; he fought rebellions, revived order, and brought dignity to the house of Xia once more.

But the Xia dynasty was not meant to linger in ancient China for long. Centuries later, under Kong Jia, who reigned circa 1789 BCE, the dynasty began to see the beginning of its end. Kong Jia was often depicted as a heavy drinker, often forgetting his responsibilities. His successors, Gao and Fa, were also remembered for neglecting their subjects. The final ruler from the Xia dynasty was Jie (traditionally dated from 1728 BCE to 1675 BCE). A tyrant whose cruelty pushed away both his allies and subjects, Jie was eventually left with no choice but to face a rebellion near the end of his rule. The uprising was led by a certain Tang of Shang, who overthrew Jie and ended the Xia dynasty by establishing the Shang dynasty.

Now, the question remains: did the Xia truly exist? Unlike the Shang and Zhou, whose inscriptions and records survived the test of time, the Xia left us with no contemporary writings. In fact, the story of Yu taming the floods, founding the dynasty, and passing the throne to his son carries the unmistakable shape of myth. Some viewed this narrative as an origin story that embodies virtue and order rather than a precise chronicle of events.

Archaeology complicates the tale further. Excavations at Erlitou, in Henan province, reveal a thriving Bronze Age culture dated roughly between 1900 and 1500 BCE. Palaces once stood there, bronze casting flourished, and a stratified society wielded significant power. This led scholars to suggest that Erlitou was once the very capital of the Xia dynasty. However, this was a matter of debate. Some scholars disagree with the suggestion, especially when no inscriptions or text have been found that connect the city to the Xia.

These scholars argue that Xia may be a later invention created by historians during the Zhou and Han dynasties, who sought to legitimize dynastic succession and the Mandate of Heaven. By creating a "first dynasty" to precede the Shang, they could frame their own rule as part of an unbroken chain of heaven's chosen rulers. The pro-historic view, however, suggests that the Xia dynasty was real, corresponding to Erlitou or a similar early state but lost to us in the absence of direct inscriptions.

There is no exact answer to this question. The existence of the Xia dynasty is neither a confirmed myth, like the underwater city of Atlantis, nor confirmed history like the Shang and Zhou. It rests instead in the gray zone between memory and archaeology, legend and fact: perhaps a real Bronze Age kingdom, perhaps a story shaped to fit the needs of later generations.

The Expedition for Immortality

With the entirety of China in his hands, Qin Shi Huang was left with one last adversary that he could neither conquer nor bend to his will. This enemy was none other than death itself.

Each day, the emperor wrestled with the thought that, despite having conquered even the fiercest kingdom of all, he too would soon be a victim of death. He had already survived two murder attempts; sooner or later, his luck would certainly run out. So, he consulted his trusted advisors, ministers, and generals about immortality, yet none had the knowledge. He then turned to his physicians and alchemists, all of whom were well versed in the realm of health and medicine. Under the emperor's order, these men of science began experiments. They spent day and night in their laboratories, mixing strange minerals into potions. They experimented with various rare herbs, yet none of these human-made concoctions could loosen death's grip.

Then, the emperor heard rumors of a place believed to be the answer to his trouble. They spoke of three islands that lay hidden somewhere in the eastern seas. These lands were named Penglai, Fangzhang, and Yingzhou and were described as an enchanted paradise where immortals roamed. One of these immortals was named Anqi Sheng. He lived on Mount Penglai and, according to legend, was nearing a thousand years old by the time Qin Shi Huang rose as emperor. On Penglai, one could also find a type of fruit whispered to have the ability to cure any ailment and grant eternal youth to those who consumed it. Some even claimed it could restore life to the dead.

To an emperor who was unwilling to yield to time, it was a must to uncover whether the island existed. Without wasting a moment, Qin Shi Huang launched an expedition eastward, hoping his subjects could return with the enchanted fruit or perhaps an elixir of immortality.

The said expedition was spearheaded by the emperor's court alchemist, Xu Fu. He left the empire sometime in 219 BCE, crossing the relentless ocean and battling through unpredictable weather. Qin Shi Huang made it clear that failure was not an option. Yet, the expedition unfortunately ended in disappointment. Whether beaten back by storms or simply unable to locate the island, Xu Fu had no other choice but to return empty-handed. When questioned by the emperor, he knew that he should not speak the truth. Otherwise, his life would be on the line.

Therefore, the alchemist conjured a story, one involving a sea beast prowling the ocean. He spoke of how the expedition was forced to halt because they were unable to cross without alerting the beast. Shi Huang Di then dispatched his archers to eliminate the creature. When they returned, claiming that they had succeeded in clearing the way, Xu Fu was ordered to embark on a second expedition to the mysterious island.

A Japanese illustration of Xu Fu's voyage.[18]

Another version—rather high in myth—told a different story in which Xu Fu did find the island during his first expedition. When he asked the guardian of the island for the elixir of life, the mysterious immortal told him to come back with offerings.

"Bring me the sons of good families and beautiful maidens," the guardian may have instructed Xu Fu, "along with the products of your various craftsmen. Then only will I permit you to bring the elixir to your master!"

Exaggerations and legends aside, Xu Fu set out on the second expedition on a larger scale. The alchemist brought a total of three thousand men, women, and children on board along with many provisions, seeds, silks, and supplies. However, like his first expedition, Xu Fu failed to find the mystical island. He knew that to return to the empire meant certain death since the emperor would never tolerate failure, especially when it came to his obsession with immortality. Therefore, Xu Fu chose to disappear. The famed alchemist never returned, and that was the last time anyone had ever heard of him and his entire crew.

While it is uncertain where exactly he went, there are suspicions that Xu Fu eventually found Mount Penglai, though to us it is known as Mount Fuji, Japan. Here, the alchemist and the rest of his crew made themselves at home. They introduced new skills to the local people. Among this knowledge was none other than the cultivation of rice, which later became the backbone of Japanese agriculture.

Coincidentally, this legend aligns with what we know from Japanese history. Archaeological evidence places the spread of wet rice cultivation into Japan around the same period, brought over from the Asian mainland during the late Yayoi era. Interestingly, the Japanese themselves came to hold Xu Fu in high regard. In some regions, he was revered as a culture-bringer, a wise sage from across the sea who brought not only the techniques of rice cultivation but also valuable knowledge of medicine, sericulture (silk farming), and new tools. The Japanese even erected shrines, and his statue can be found to this day at Jofuku Park. While we cannot say with certainty that Xu Fu himself was responsible for spreading this knowledge, the timing is close enough to make us think the story may hold at least a few grains of truth.

Chapter 6 – Tragedies of Injustice

Justice in ancient China was never a matter taken lightly. From the earliest days of the Zhou dynasty, the law was viewed not merely as a human system but as an extension of cosmic order. To disturb harmony within the family or the state was to disturb the balance of heaven itself. Legal codes were already strict, and punishments could be harsh. Records tell of a Zhou noble punished severely for a crime that today might seem trivial: he allowed his employees to mistreat peasants under his watch. The court ruled that because he had failed in his duty to protect the weak, his own life was forfeited. Such cases showed how justice was often more about preserving hierarchy and stability than about fairness to the individual.

Then came the Qin and Han dynasties. With their Legalist ideas, this principle was strengthened. Laws were codified and punishments standardized. Often, officials ruled through fear as much as reason. In theory, this created an orderly society where crime was deterred. But, in practice, the weight of the law often fell unevenly. A wealthy merchant could walk free after bribing the right people, while a poor farmer could face the cruelest punishment for petty crimes.

This gave rise to some of the most tragic stories in Chinese history. These were moments when justice did not prevail. These were episodes when innocence was punished and guilt went unscathed. They were tales that horrified contemporaries and have since been remembered for centuries, passed down as warnings of the dangers of unchecked authority.

The Exiled Advisor

There was once a man named Qu Yuan who lived in the state of Chu sometime during the fourth century BCE when China was still struggling through the Warring States period. Born into a noble family, Qu Yuan enjoyed privilege. He rose to prominence as a minister in his twenties, and his main responsibility was advising King Huai of Chu.

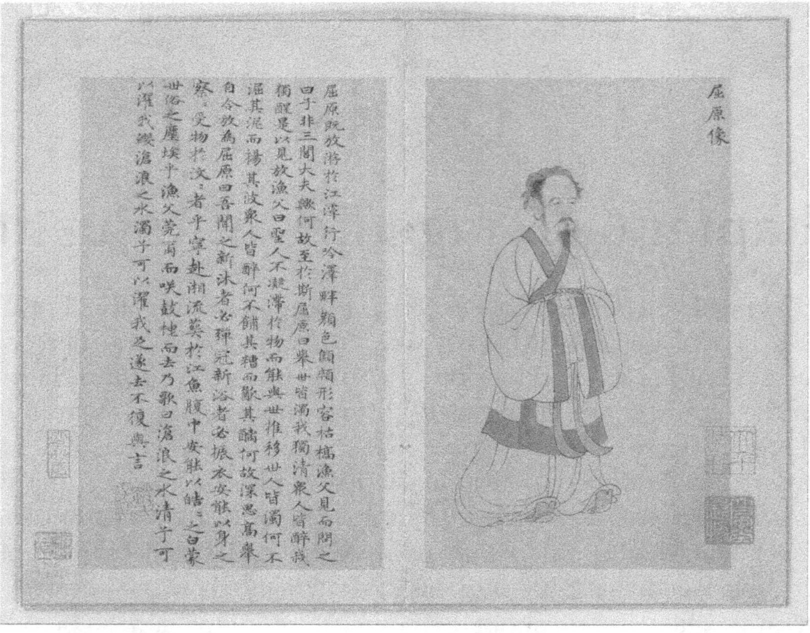

Qu Yuan, depicted in the Nine Songs (an ancient set of poems).[19]

Qu Yuan deserved the position. He was not like the other courtiers. He was well educated, eloquent, and cunning. He was always a step ahead, constantly strategizing for the benefit of his homeland. And so, Qu Yuan was quick to notice the danger that the state of Qin would soon bring, especially as it was rapidly growing. He knew that division and mistrust between the other states would invite total destruction once Qin chose to advance more boldly. Thus, Qu Yuan did not hesitate to urge King Huai to form alliances with other kingdoms like Qi, Han, and Zhao to effectively counterbalance Qin's aggression.

He also pressed for reforms within Chu, advising the king to strengthen the state's administration. As someone who saw the importance of peace and prosperity among not only the nobles but also the common folk, Qu Yuan also worked to ensure the common people were treated fairly.

But the royal court was a dangerous field full of betrayal and dishonesty. Certainly, the king valued him. His ideals and integrity initially made him a favorite, and he was entrusted with drafting decrees and shaping policies. But his virtues did not sit well with everyone. Many, especially those who thrived on flattery and intrigue, were envious of his position and achievement. They detested his honesty. Seeking to enrich themselves, these jealous ministers soon began to plot.

Exactly what the ministers said was never disclosed, but it is safe to assume that their slander included the claim that Qu Yuan was growing too proud and that his insistence on moral uprightness was twisted into arrogance. They may have also suggested how Qu Yuan often looked down on the king's judgment, implying that he, the advisor, thought himself wiser than his sovereign. They also spoke of fear, claiming that Qu Yuan was so dangerously close to the common people that this could turn into a rival power base that challenged the king's authority.

King Huai eventually fell for the slander. This marked the beginning of Qu Yuan's fall. He was later stripped of his office, pushed away from court, and finally exiled from the capital of Chu. Despite giving his life to service, Qu Yuan was thrown out in the blink of an eye. This betrayal cut deep, yet he continued to live—at least for a while. He wandered the countryside and was only allowed to watch from afar as the kingdom he loved slowly journeyed toward its destruction under poor counsel.

It was during this time of exile that Qu Yuan turned to literature. He lamented his fate in his most famous work, called *Li Sao.* He wrote of his dream and despair, expressing both his devotion to the kingdom and his sorrow at its corruption. He likened himself to a fragrant herb in a field of weeds, clinging to integrity while others thrived through deceit.

A few years later, his nightmare turned into reality. Qin's strength had grown tremendously. Its armies were beyond disciplined and would stop at nothing until their king could have every land in his grasp. The state of Chu, on the other hand, was on the brink of collapse. Its alliances had faltered, and the court was panicking. King Huai himself was captured in 299 BCE after being tricked into attending a conference in Qin. He escaped two years later, only to be recaptured once more. He died in 296 BCE, still in the captivity of Qin. Chu was then put under the helm of his son, King Qingxiang, though he fared no better. The king continued to heed corrupt voices and dismissed those who would have saved the kingdom.

It was said that Qu Yuan shouted warnings once more, but as expected, they went unheeded. Overwhelmed with despair, he wandered to the banks of the Miluo River. Losing purpose in life, knowing that he could no longer serve his homeland, Qu Yuan threw himself into the river.

Word of his drowning shocked the people, who wept for his fate. The story goes that fishermen in the area immediately abandoned their catch and rowed their boats toward the place where Qu Yuan had drowned. They rowed back and forth as they beat drums, splashing their oars to frighten fish and evil spirits away, but they never discovered his remains. Over the centuries, this grief transformed into tradition. The dragon boat races held every year on the fifth day of the fifth lunar month mirror the episode when the people of Chu scoured the river for Qu Yuan's body.

Pursued, Celebrated, and Condemned All Over Again

Wu Zixu too was born into the state of Chu, though he lived during the restless years of the Spring and Autumn period, centuries before Qu Yuan. He belonged to a noble family, where his father, Wu She, served as a minister. His life changed when a minister named Fei Wuji slandered his father and elder brother, accusing them of disloyalty. As a result, they were sentenced to death. Wu Zixu, who was still young at the time, fled the kingdom, as the king had dispatched soldiers to eradicate his entire family.

Branded as the son of a traitor, Wu Zixu was left alone and hunted. He made his way to the west, never once revealing his real name to anyone he encountered. He crossed rivers, living on scraps, and spent his nights awake, fearing capture. A certain legend spoke of the time when he was nearly captured by his pursuers. When he reached the Huai River, Wu Zixu hid among the reeds. He was then discovered by a certain fisherman who asked his name. He never answered, but the fisherman guessed his identity. Claiming that Wu Zixu's destiny was not yet complete, the fisherman assisted his escape.

His destiny brought him to the kingdom of Wu, where he managed to secure a position under Prince Guang—later known as King Helü of Wu. Perhaps knowing that it was better to remain honest, Wu Zixu informed the prince of his past. He even included the part where he sought vengeance against the king of Chu for murdering his family.

A copy of Sun Tzu's Art of War, written on bamboo.[20]

When the prince seized the throne, Wu Zixu remained loyal. He became the king's most trusted counselor. Together with the famed strategist, Sun Tzu (known best as the author of *The Art of War*), Wu Zixu played a hand in pushing the kingdom into its golden age of military power. Wu Zixu's knowledge of Chu's terrain and politics also made him invaluable. For years, he bided his time, waiting for the right moment to strike at the state that had once wronged his family.

That time came in 506 BCE, when King Helü, urged by both Wu Zixu and Sun Tzu, decided to launch a major campaign against Chu. Wu Zixu, driven by both vengeance and the desire to display his undying loyalty to his new king, led the charge. Utilizing the ruthless and precise Wu armies, Wu Zixu succeeded in crushing the enemy and storming their capital, Ying. Panicked, King Zhao of Chu abandoned his throne and made an escape.

However, Wu Zixu was not particularly interested in the fleeing king. He was now standing in the very palace where his family had been condemned. Without hesitation, he demanded that the tomb of King Ping of Chu, the one who was responsible for executing his father and brother, be opened. To Wu Zixu, revenge could be served even to the dead. And so, he had the corpse of King Ping exhumed and flogged. Some might see this action as desecration, but to Wu Zixu, this was retribution.

In the aftermath of Chu's defeat, Wu Zixu continued to play a decisive role in Wu's affairs. In 495 BCE, Wu emerged victorious over Yue at the Battle of Fujiao. This resulted in the submission of the king of Yue, Goujian, and seemed like the end of Yue. Wu Zixu, however, saw differently. He warned the court that Goujian's submission was nothing more than an act, a way for him to buy time. Unfortunately, none heeded his caution.

When Helü died from wounds he sustained in a battle against Yue, the throne was handed to his son, Fuchai. Again, Wu Zixu repeated his warning but with an even greater urgency. He pressured the new king of Wu to annihilate Yue completely instead of turning his ambitions elsewhere. Wu Zixu was certain that sparing Goujian would one day prove disastrous. But Fuchai was young and naive. Upon listening to the poisonous words of a courtier named Bo Pi—who was said to have been bribed by the Yue—Fuchai chose to spare Goujian. Believing that he had no intention to rebel against Wu, the king sent him back to his kingdom.

Wu Zixu's vision was beginning to turn into reality. While King Fuchai turned his gaze elsewhere, eager to realize his ambition of claiming hegemony among the Chinese states, Goujian was busy preparing for revenge. Wu Zixu pressed for Fuchai to consolidate and crush Yue while they still had the upper hand. But the king refused to listen. Irritated, Fuchai eventually saw Wu Zixu as an obstacle rather than an ally. Hence, in 484 BCE, the king ordered the loyal minister to take his own life.

As his final request, Wu Zixu asked that his eyes be gouged out and hung upon the eastern gate of the capital. This way, even in death, the minister could witness the destruction of the kingdom he had once so strongly protected.

Years later, his warnings came to pass. Goujian rose against Wu and exploited Fuchai's complacency. This shattered Wu's strength, and in 473 BCE, the kingdom fell. Fuchai, cornered and defeated, committed suicide.

From Friends to Enemies

This story begins with a friendship. Pan Juan and Sun Bin were students of the legendary strategist, Gui Guzi. Under his tutelage, the two studied the art of war in seclusion, taking in lessons that could shape the destinies of kingdoms. Although they were friends, they had different traits and personalities. While Pang Juan was the more ambitious one, always eager to apply what he had learned to achieve glory, Sun Bin was more reserved. He was brilliant but always remembered to temper it with humility. However, when it was made clear that Sun Bin's talent was superior to his, Pang Juan began to develop a hint of jealousy—which would grow as time passed.

Pang Juan wasted no time crafting a path of success for himself. He sought out military service in Wei and rose through the ranks rather quickly, becoming a general under King Hui. After achieving a list of victories, Pang Juan was elevated to the position of commander. Even though he had achieved so much, insecurity still lingered in his heart. Although Sun Bin had not yet achieved prominence, Pang Juan could not live with the thought that his old classmate would soon eclipse him. Perhaps it was better to silence the threat before it could even manifest. Therefore, he invited Pang Juan to the capital of Wei, pretending he was ecstatic for a reunion.

The unsuspecting Sun Bin accepted the invitation. He was welcomed warmly and showered with honor as a guest. This, of course, was only an act. Pang Juan then laid accusations against his old friend. He claimed that Sun Bin harbored intentions to destroy the kingdom of Wei. As a result, terrible punishments were ordered. Sun Bin was seized and subjected to *xing*, the removal of the kneecaps. But crippling him was not enough. His face was also tattooed with the mark of shame, branding him as a traitor.

Sun Bin was imprisoned and put under close watch at all times. He knew there was no way out unless he could prove that he was incapable of harming the state. So, he feigned madness. Sun Bin started scribbling nonsense on the walls, ranting incoherently, and waking the guards up at odd hours by laughing uncontrollably. Over time, his captors lowered their guard, believing that he was truly insane and harmless.

This was an opportunity for the envoys from Qi. Early on, they had heard of a crippled prisoner who was a brilliant strategist. After investigating the rumor, they eventually agreed that Sun Bin was indeed a man worth saving. The envoys secretly smuggled him out of Wei and brought him to Qi, where he later found a new purpose as the kingdom's respected military strategist.

It did not take long for Sun Bin to cross paths with his envious friend again. Led by his old classmate, the forces of Wei were besieging the capital of Zhou, Handan. When Zhou turned to Qi for help, Sun Bin knew this was the moment he had patiently been waiting for. Knowing it was unwise to go against a raging opponent head-on, Sun Bin feigned weakness. He intentionally launched an unsuccessful attack against Wei elsewhere, convincing the enemy that the Qi were not strong enough to defeat them.

Upon learning about the defeat of Qi, Pang Juan called for more troops from Daliang to continue besieging Handan. These troops left the Wei capital nearly unprotected. Seeing that his plans were going well, Sun Bin led an army to the capital city, prompting Pang Juan to make a mad dash to save Daliang. He was in such a rush that he left his infantry and supplies at Handan, taking only his cavalry with him. Since they were riding at full speed, Pang Juan's men fell into exhaustion just as they crossed the Yellow River. Little did they know, Sun Bin was already waiting for them with a large army. An ambush was launched, and Sun Bin emerged victorious. Pang Juan, his reputation now tarnished, managed to retreat.

The two former friends faced each other once more in 342 BCE at the Battle of Maling. Again, Sun Bin came up with a ruse to defeat the enemy. He ordered the Qi army to light fewer and fewer cooking fires each day so that the enemy would think his troops were deserting. Pang Juan fell for the tactic. Eager to crush Sun Bin and perhaps restore his image, the Wei general rushed his forces forward through a narrow valley at night. Unbeknownst to the Wei forces, they had entered a trap.

As Pang Juan and his men passed through, dozens of Qi archers fired at them, decimating as many men as possible. Later, Qi infantry poured in, fighting the enemy in close combat. Some said Pang Juan was among those who fell to the arrows, while others claimed he survived but then commit suicide.

Legend has it that, despite having claimed victory and exacted revenge on the man responsible for his unjust punishments years prior, Sun Bin was sad the moment he saw the body of his former friend. As for Wei, the kingdom was thrown into a deeper chasm, never to return to its glory ever again. Although the kingdom lingered for more than a century, Wei was left vulnerable to the pressures of not only Qi but also Qin on the west.

The Punished Historian

The name Sima Qian may be familiar, especially to those who have read the story of ancient China. However, long before his name rose to prominence, there was his father, known as Sima Tan. He served as the grand astrologer, an important position in the Han dynasty that demanded more than just watching the stars; his duties also included recording the annals of the empire to keep track of rituals, omens, and most importantly, the deeds of the mighty rulers and ministers. Of course, his work was not simply a matter of compiling names and dates. He was expected to ensure that the story of China endured through centuries, if not millennia.

Sima Tan was aware of the weight of this responsibility, but he embraced it wholeheartedly. History was his passion, and he had long dreamed of being given this very opportunity. He believed that such work should not only preserve the past but also teach the present and guide the future. However, fate had another story for him. Sima Tan contracted a life-endangering illness. Knowing that he would never realize his ambition, he called for his son, Sima Qian.

"The responsibility now rests upon your shoulders," he may have said as he entrusted his son with a final request. "Promise me that you will finish what I have begun."

Sima Tan died in 110 BCE, leaving all his scrolls and notes to his son. Wishing to honor his father, Sima Qian devoted himself to the history of China. He traveled widely across the land, searching for stories and events that shaped the empire. He visited ancient battlefields where soil was once soaked in blood, walked through palaces that witnessed coronations and assassinations, and sought the wisdom of elders who still remembered the events of past reigns.

A portrait of Sima Qian.[21]

At a glance, the life of a historian seemed far safer than that of a soldier who was expected to brave arrows from afar and blades at close quarters. But Sima Qian's story proves otherwise. It all began with Emperor Wu of Han, who was famously ruling with an iron hand. He had launched many violent expansion campaigns, which eventually drained the treasury and robbed his land of countless lives. It is not surprising to learn that his court was filled with suspicion, and those who dared to speak words out of step with imperial judgment could easily see the end of their lives.

The campaign that sealed Sima Qian's fate was the one involving the nomadic Xiongnu. Ever ambitious and eager to heighten his power, Emperor Wu launched a campaign led by his own brother-in-law, Li Guangli, who was supported by another general, Li Ling. With the support of one hundred thousand men, Li Guangli wasted no time marching north. However, the journey was perilous; the northern steppes were difficult to navigate, especially with the windswept plains. The Xiongnu, on the other hand, knew the land well. With this advantage, the nomads struck at their enemy swiftly and vanished quickly into the wilderness before the Han forces could react.

It did not take long for Li Guangli to realize that his usual strategy would not work on the Xiongnu. He began the campaign full of confidence, and his mistake was a simple one: he did not anticipate the speed and cunning of his enemy. His army withered faster than he could have imagined. In the end, of the hundred thousand men that marched into the north, only ten thousand limped back. His defeat was so humiliating that, at first, he was refused re-entry into Han territory. But the emperor was unwilling to admit failure on the part of his own kin. Hence, he needed a scapegoat.

That scapegoat was none other than General Li Ling. While Li Guangli commanded a large force, Li Ling had only five thousand infantry. Despite this small number, Li Ling went on against the Xiongnu, fighting them off for weeks. He and his men moved across the difficult terrain and never hesitated to stand against impossible odds. They fought the enemy bravely; his archers used up every last one of their arrows, and the rest fought until their blades were either blunted or fell from their hands. While they managed to cut down thousands of enemies, the Xiongnu outnumbered them. They could only win if somehow the gods descended from the heavens and intervened. And so, surrounded and exhausted, with his resources dwindling, Li Ling made the choice to surrender. It was an act of compassion rather than cowardice: the general did so to save what was left of his men from being slaughtered.

When news of this surrender reached the emperor, he was furious. But, at the same time, it gave him the scapegoat he needed. Thus, the emperor branded Li Ling a traitor. Although not everyone in court agreed with the condemnation, none of them dared to voice their opinion, for whoever questioned the Son of Heaven would certainly face dire consequences.

This was when Sima Qian entered the story. He rose in defense of Li Ling. He argued that the general had fought with unmatched valor. With only five thousand men, he had achieved what armies ten times that size could not. He exclaimed that the surrender was not an act of betrayal but a sacrifice for his soldiers.

His words, however, enraged Emperor Wu even more. The Son of Heaven reacted by arresting Sima Qian and throwing him into the palace prison. He subjected the historian to a death sentence by suicide. Sima Qian sat in his cell, staring at the cold stone walls, confronted with the end. Yet the promise he had made to his father, and the unfinished history he had dedicated his life to, gnawed at him. He was not ready to let it die with him.

Sima Qian's tomb and ancestral temple in Hancheng.[22]

He learned that there were two possible alternatives to escape the death penalty. The first option was to purchase a commutation into exile. Of course, such mercy came at a steep price, and unfortunately for Sima Qian, he did not have enough wealth. This left him with the second option, which was castration. This was considered the lowest degradation. To go through a castration meant that he would be plunged into a life of humiliation, derision, and contempt. He would certainly get cast out of respectable society. He would never get a chance to have a family and would be branded a scourge upon humanity. Many would rather end their lives than living with such disgrace.

But not Sima Qian. To die was to betray his father's dying wish. Thus, he chose to live. With this, Sima Qian was dragged, bound, and mutilated in 99 BCE. He was not the only one to go through this punishment. Alongside him was Li Ling, also cast into disgrace.

When he was released from prison, Sima Qian immediately experienced a change in his life. His friends no longer greeted him warmly. Instead, they avoided him altogether. His colleagues and even strangers looked at him in disgust. He was officially a living shame. Sima Qian wrote to his friend, Ren An, expressing how he felt. He talked about the unbearable shame he had to endure each time he stepped outside and the endless nights of contemplating suicide.

But his father's legacy demanded he live. This was possibly the sole reason he continued to wake up each morning. Despite the torment, he bent himself back to the brush. Eventually, out of this disgrace came the *Shiji*. Completed in 91 BCE, it consisted of a hundred and thirty chapters and spanned two thousand years, from the age of the Yellow Emperor to the reign of Emperor Wu. The author himself died in 86 BCE only a few years following the completion of his greatest work.

Chapter 7 – The Favorites

The practice of keeping concubines was not something new in the long history of ancient China. The practice traces its roots to many centuries ago, stretching back to the feudal courts of the Zhou and the Warring States period. During these turbulent times, rulers often accepted daughters of noble houses as concubines in the name of alliance. Then came the unification of China under the Qin in 221 BCE. From then on, concubinage changed. It moved from a regional custom to an imperial institution.

Since he was considered the supreme ruler of everything under heaven, the emperor was expected to preside over a harem that reflected both his power and the breadth of his empire. After all, this system of concubines ensured a constant supply of heirs should the dynasty need them. Hence, concubines were brought into the palace from across the realm. Some were given as tributes from noble houses. while others were chosen by officials after going through selection processes. Some were also taken as the spoils of war.

According to Sima Qian, Emperor Qin Shi Huang himself maintained a harem of about ten thousand women. Scholars, however, agree that this number was meant to be a rhetorical exaggeration; in ancient Chinese writing, "ten thousand" was often used to describe something beyond measure. Interestingly, despite having a harem and being married twice, Qin Shi Huang never elevated a consort to the rank of empress; he remains the only Chinese emperor in history never to have named an empress.

The reasons behind this remain a mystery, though some have pointed to his troubled past. His mother was said to have had a scandalous affair with a merchant-turned-politician named Lü Buwei and later a man referred to as Lao Ai. Perhaps these liaisons and the political conspiracies surrounding them scarred the young ruler, who in turn, associated women with betrayal, deception, and the dangers of divided loyalty. Another reason lay in his self-image. It is plausible that the emperor saw himself as not only a monarch but also a powerful figure who had surpassed all who came before. After all, he had a long list of achievements. To appoint an empress would have been to elevate one woman above thousands, granting her symbolic parity in the cosmic order. For a ruler who considered himself unmatched, perhaps no woman seemed worthy to stand at his side.

By the Han dynasty, concubinage had become one of the pillars of imperial life. The difference was that it was no longer a loose collection of women around the emperor but an institution as rigid and stratified as the bureaucracy itself. Concubinage in this period even had its own hierarchy. At the top was none other than the empress (*huanghou*). Below her were nine ranks of consorts, each given a title that symbolized her prestige. These different titles also dictated nearly every aspect of the concubine's life, from the number of attendants she was entitled to the silks she wore and even the dishes served at her table.

A concubine could be visited by the emperor and shared a bed with the Son of Heaven, yet this did not shield her from any danger that lurked behind the palace walls. To be in the lowest rank of the hierarchy meant she could end up being alone—many concubines never even had the honor of meeting the emperor—but being the ultimate favorite was equally dangerous. Jealousy and coups often took place among the concubines as these women vied for the emperor's affection. The story of Lady Qi, for instance, gives clear insight into the competition and jealousy that constantly existed in the emperor's harem.

A Peking opera actress portraying Wang Zhaojun, one of the Four Beauties of ancient China and the concubine of Emperor Yuan of Han.[28]

With the emergence of the Tang dynasty, concubinage again expanded into something grander. The Tang court was famed for its cosmopolitan brilliance. Hence, it is not surprising that it ritualized the harem into an immense hierarchy of one hundred and twenty-two ranks.

For aristocratic families, offering a daughter to the emperor was both an honor and a political strategy. Since these women were highborn and offered in the name of alliance, they were given an entrance that was far from humble. They did not have to start from the bottom of the hierarchy but were granted a high rank from the beginning. The rest, however, could only secure a place in the palace through a more formal selection process.

When it was time to supply the emperor with new concubines, the court would issue an edict to "select beauties" (*xuanxiu*). Then, officials from Chang'an would be dispatched throughout the provinces to identify suitable candidates. However, not everyone fell under their radar; the officials would only look for candidates from what were called *liángjiāzǐ* (respectable households), usually in their mid-teens. Oftentimes, their eyes would be fixed on daughters of lower-ranking officials. Those born into families of merchants and artisans were excluded outright since these professions were located at the bottom of the hierarchy. The families of the chosen candidates—typically the fathers—were then given a summon for their daughters to appear at Chang'an for the next step.

Of course, to refuse an invitation by the court would certainly mean punishment. But the candidates were not expected to travel at their own expense. Typically, the provincial officials would send covered carriages or palanquins to the girls. They would depart to the capital accompanied by attendants and guards. As for their families, this scene was both an honor and a loss. Should their daughters pass all the inspections and tests, this would be the last time they would lay eyes on them. Concubines were not permitted to leave the palace grounds and could only meet their family under emergencies, though this was only permitted in extremely rare, supervised occasions. In return for their daughters, the families would be compensated with gifts—usually silk, money, or official promotions for the fathers and brothers.

Once they arrived at Chang'an, the candidates must go through an imperial audition. This was a series of trials that stripped away the last remnants of their old identity. First, the girls must go through the physical inspection. They were examined head to toe, typically by the eunuchs. These were the loyal servants of the emperor, most of whom had been castrated as boys. Some were sold by desperate families; others volunteered in the hope of rising to influence. (Eunuchs, too, had ranks and departments, and their roles could range from menial servants to some of the most powerful figures in court.)

Apart from teeth and hair, their posture was also measured and their skin checked. Even the smallest blemish could immediately result in dismissal, let alone a limp or a scar. Of course, their physical appearance was not the only thing that was important. The next stage involved a virginity examination. While later folklore spoke of mystical signs like the "gecko cinnabar" mark that supposedly revealed whether a woman had known a man, the palace relied on invasive examinations. Medical knowledge at the time associated virginity with certain physical signs, particularly the presence of an intact hymen. The task of determining virginity was placed onto senior maids or female physicians who would probe and prod the candidates.

A woman who failed the inspection would be dismissed and returned to her family. This might sound simple, yet for her family, it was a shame. No matter how trivial the reasons behind her dismissal were, being rejected by the palace could invite whispers that she was "tainted." However, sometimes rejected candidates were reassigned into lesser palace service such as that of a maid or attendant.

Those who passed moved on to the test of refinement and grace. Every bow, every glance, every word was observed by experienced eyes. The way she held her hands, the way she lowered her gaze, the rhythm of her steps, all were judged in the most critical way possible. A single awkward gesture could portray her as unworthy. The tension of this stage was undoubtedly almost unbearable, for it was not enough to be beautiful. To pass, a candidate had to appear naturally graceful, effortlessly poised, and innately suited to the rarefied air of the palace. Many girls faltered at this stage, undone not by lack of beauty but by nerves, if not clumsiness.

The remaining candidates were put to yet another challenge, which involved showcasing their talent. The Tang emperors were known to be patrons of culture, often surrounding themselves with sophisticated poets, musicians, and artists. Hence, it is not surprising that they demanded their companions reflect that refinement. One of the girls might be asked to compose a poem right there and then; her choice of words alone could either secure her a position in the Forbidden City or doom her future entirely. Some might be given a brush to paint a scene, their elegance in each stroke judged critically. Others might be told to play a melody, their tunes judged for both technical perfection and emotional resonance. This was the time for a girl of more modest looks than others to shine. Her gifts in poetry, painting, or music could enchant the judges far more than a flawless beauty who could only smile.

With the end of the trials, officials would come up with a list of finalists. Sometimes, the list was handed to the emperor, who would review the girls. But often the decisions were made by his senior consorts, the empress dowager, or his most trusted eunuchs. The lives of the girls who were accepted as concubines experienced a swift transformation. Officials would notify their families and reward them with lavish gifts. However, they could no longer see their daughters. From this moment on, their old ties were cut. It seemed as if the girls ceased to be daughters. Given the title *cǎinǚ* (selected lady), they were officially in the possession of the emperor.

Never again would they taste poverty; the concubines were showered with luxury. Yet, some viewed their lives differently: they were living in a prison. They could not leave. They could not marry because they were reserved strictly for the emperor. Yet, many would never even get a glimpse of the Son of Heaven, forced to spend their days waiting for a summons that never came. Loneliness was their only company. As for those who were fortunate enough to gain his attention, their nights would not be so lonely. They could even rise rapidly through the ranks. However, they also must always be cautious. Earning too much attention from the emperor could also be dangerous. Other concubines might be envious enough to plan sabotage. An envious concubine might bribe a eunuch or an attendant into her devious plans just so she could watch the other girl crumble.

The concubinage system endured for many centuries, even after the Tang. Later dynasties formalized the process still further, scheduling selections that swept in girls from every province and refining the ranks until the harem became a state within a state. Some concubines rose to rule empires as empresses, while others lived a far quieter life, their names lost even to history. The system lingered until the last days of the Qing and was only abolished in 1949 with the founding of the People's Republic.

The Emperor's Male Favorites

While the story of imperial concubinage in ancient China usually revolved around women, there were times when emperors had other favorites. Interestingly, the Sons of Heaven did not always confine their desires to women alone. Hints of same-sex affections at court appear as early as the Spring and Autumn period, though these stories were often overshadowed. To modern eyes, this may seem contradictory, especially to the patriarchal system of ancient China. But the reality was more nuanced.

This was a time when emperors were considered above all. They were expected to uphold Confucian ideals. Emperors must honor their ancestors, ensure the continuity of their lineage, and produce heirs to secure the dynasty. As long as these obligations were fulfilled, their private affections were their own business. Especially in the Han dynasty (a period when stories of male concubines are more apparent), there were no prohibitions against same-sex intimacy. Hence, there was no moral panic about it or any stigma of illegality. Criticism would only surface when a male favorite wielded undue influence. It would only cause an uproar if his presence distracted the emperor completely, taking him away from affairs of state and the mission of providing heirs.

In contrast to the female consorts, male concubines had no official structure or harem reserved for them. Instead, they were known only by an informal term, *nán chŏng*, which literally means "male favorite" or "male concubine." In short, a male favorite's entire existence and privileges depended strictly on the emperor's affection. If a certain young man managed to maintain favor with the Son of Heaven, he might enjoy influence and wealth beyond anything his birth could have provided. But his influence, status, and wealth were never guaranteed. Unlike female concubines who still belonged to the emperor even after his death (though their life was essentially gilded captivity), the position of a male favorite could vanish overnight if he lost favor or the emperor simply died.

This lack of an institutional framework is what made the role of a male concubine both dangerous and unique. Sometimes, the impact of a male favorite could extend far beyond the emperor's bedchamber. Emperor Hui of Han, for instance, was believed to be enamored by a young man named Hong Ru. One of the few ways to get on the emperor's good side was to mirror the tastes of the man he favored. Hence, Hong Ru's personal style turned into fashion, and court officials began imitating his looks. They added feathers in their hats and lightly powdered their faces. Some even wore ornaments dangling from their robes just like the young lover.

Since the path to becoming a male concubine was far less formalized compared to that of imperial women, how exactly could one stumble upon such a destiny? The answer lay in chances: a man could find himself elevated to the intimate circle of the emperor not by design but by chance. Before becoming a male concubine, one could be a low-ranking official or even an entertainer who once performed a song or recited a poem before the Son of Heaven. Eunuchs, too, sometimes found themselves crossing the line from servant to companion. What mattered was not lineage or a family's political ambition but the man's abilities to enchant the emperor with his looks or perhaps wit.

It is safe to conclude that these male concubines were not confined to a gilded cage. While their counterparts had to leave their families behind once selected by the emperor, a male favorite was allowed to maintain his own household outside the palace walls. He could even marry a woman, raise children, and build a family since he was not technically absorbed into a harem system. His relationship with the emperor, however, could leave an impact on his family in terms of fortune. Once a male concubine was favored, the emperor often showered his family with gifts, land, and even opportunities to hold court positions.

Of all the Han emperors, the one known to be closely associated with male concubines was Emperor Wu. He was known for his long reign—he sat on the Dragon Throne for over five decades—and martial prowess. It was under Emperor Wu that the Han dynasty achieved its greatest territorial expansion; the empire stretched from the Fergana Valley in the west to northern Korea in the east and northern Vietnam in the south. With all those years on the throne and his vast achievements, the emperor was constantly surrounded by courtiers and officials. Among all, one of the few who stood closest to him was known as Han Yan.

According to the *Shiji* and the *Book of Han*, the two had already known each other for years, back to when the emperor was referred to by his name, Liu Che. Both Han Yan and Liu Che shared calligraphy lessons when they were young. Details of their early days are scarce, but many historians agree that it was this early companionship that planted the seeds of a closeness that eventually endured into adulthood. By the time Liu Che sat on the throne, succeeding his father, Emperor Jing in 141 BCE, Han Yan was already a familiar presence.

Emperor Wu of Han, accompanied by his two attendants.[24]

Sources claim that Han Yan was a striking character, both in appearance and ability. Indeed, ancient records describe his beauty and charm, but they also emphasize his physical skills. Han Yan was a horse whisperer; he could ride, control, and guide a steed with elegance and mastery. He was also exceptional in archery, a skill that perfectly aligned with Emperor Wu's martial inclinations. Perhaps Emperor Wu found in Han Yan a mirror of his own spirit. Sima Qian claimed that it was common for the two to rise in the morning together, hinting at the deep comfort they found in one another's company.

Of course, the emperor's favor transformed Han Yan's entire life. He was honored with gifts. Emperor Wu showered him with fine silks, jewels, horses, and all other kinds of privileges typically reserved for ministers and royal bloods. His influence at court was undoubtedly immense. Knowing he had the ear and the heart of the most powerful man in the empire, Han Yan walked with confidence. This confidence eventually turned into arrogance. Over time, the emperor's favorite began to push boundaries. He disregarded the etiquette that had long kept the imperial household in balance. The story goes that he even hunted within grounds forbidden to all except the Son of Heaven himself. However, courtiers could only voice their disapproval in silence. They knew that Han Yan had a shield and dared not invoke the wrath of the emperor.

His privilege, however, had a limit. Han Yan's downfall came when his name was mentioned in a scandal. Rumor has it that Han Yan attempted to seduce a maid. Other sources claim he was bold enough to have taken Princess Longlü, the emperor's sister, as his lover. Whichever version was true, the aftermath was the same. His action was reported, and word eventually reached the ears of Empress Dowager Xiaojing. Enraged, she made her decision, bypassing even the emperor's hesitation.

This time around, Emperor Wu's affection could not save Han Yan. He was finally summoned and ordered to take his own life.

Unsurprisingly, Han Yan was not the emperor's only male favorite. Another of his favored companions was known as Li Yannian. Unlike Han Yan, who came from the aristocracy of palace life, Li Yannian had a rather humble beginning. He was said to have committed a crime resulting in his castration. He was then made a eunuch in the palace, where he was forced to work in the royal kennels. However, his exceptional talent in the realm of music made it possible for Li Yannian to escape lowly servitude.

Some claim that Li Yannian could captivate audiences with compositions so moving that they would halt the chatter of an entire court. His melodies also managed to attract the attention of Emperor Wu. Soon, he found himself sleeping and waking up in the Son of Heaven's bedchambers. This was only the beginning of his influence in court.

Li Yannian also once performed a song titled "Jiaren Qu." The song, which he wrote himself, was about a woman whose beauty was beyond this world. Legend has it that the moment the emperor heard the song, he had a question.

"Is there truly a woman of such beauty among us?" the emperor may have asked.

The question was answered by his sister, Princess Pinyang. She told the emperor that the musician had a younger sister whose beauty was ethereal, to say the least. When Li Yannian's sister, Li Furen, was brought before the Son of Heaven, he immediately agreed that she did, in fact, matched the description sung by Li Yannian. Enthralled by her beauty, he made her his concubine.

A painting of Li Furen, after being made the emperor's concubine.[25]

This was a unique situation where a brother and sister were both loved by the emperor. Through this dual connection, Li Yannian's family rose to prominence. Apart from being one of the emperor's male lovers, Li Yannian was also given the honor of leading the re-established Imperial Music Bureau. Even Li Yannian's brother, Li Guangli, was made a general in the Han army.

Unfortunately, prosperity was not meant to linger in the Li family for long. Their influence waned when Li Furen died after giving birth to the emperor's son. Details are murky, but both Li Yannian and Li Guangli ended up being executed for treason. While some claim this was a direct result of the men having affairs with court women, others suggest their death was the work of Empress Wei Zifu, the emperor's second wife.

If Emperor Wu's favorites demonstrate how deeply personal relationships could entwine with power, the story of his grandfather, Emperor Wen, shows just how far such affection could go. In many books of history, Wen is described as a ruler of frugality and benevolence. He was remembered as a stabilizer of the Han dynasty after its turbulent founding. But even a man like Emperor Wen could be swept into devotion by chance and what he believed was divine fate.

It all began with a dream. In it, the emperor caught a glimpse of heaven high above. Yet, he struggled to ascend. He climbed up multiple times, but each time, he slipped back down. That was, however, until a mysterious man wearing a yellow hat entered the scene. He gave the Son of Heaven the push he needed to reach into the celestial realm. When Emperor Wen woke up, he was certain the dream was a sign sent by the gods.

One day, the emperor prepared for a trip. He boarded a boat and set sail along the river. A few moments later, he spotted a humble fisherman wearing the same yellow hat he had seen in his dream. He approached the man and asked for his name. Much to his surprise, the fisherman introduced himself as Deng Tong, a name that, to Chinese ears, sounded like "to ascend." This convinced the emperor that their encounter was not a mere coincidence. And so, he took the humble fisherman to his court.

Deng Tong did not step into the palace grounds as a servant but as the emperor's intimate companion. Soon, their relationship became one of devotion. When a fortune teller predicted that Deng Tong would face a grim end starving in poverty, Emperor Wen scoffed: "How can he starve, if I, the Son of Heaven, could bestow upon him all the riches this empire possesses?" He dismissed the prophecy entirely.

And with that, the emperor began granting Deng Tong vast fortunes. He even went to the extent of giving his lover the rights to control a bronze mine. Even more shocking, Deng Tong was given the privilege of minting his own coins, an authority reserved for the central government. Just a few years after their first encounter, Deng Tong's coins circulated widely, making him one of the wealthiest men in the world.

According to legend, when the emperor suffered from painful boils, it was Deng Tong who remained by his side day and night. In one of the most startling displays of devotion ever recorded, Deng Tong once placed his lips to the sores and sucked out the pus to relieve the pain. Many would consider this a grotesque act, but to Emperor Wen, this was an intimate move that proved ultimate loyalty.

"Answer me one question, Deng Tong," the emperor may have said. "Who loves me more than you?"

At first, there was silence. Bowing his head, Deng Tong answered: "No one, apart from the crown prince."

His reply was bold. It placed him alongside the heir in the emperor's affections. But Emperor Wen's love for Deng Tong grew deeply, much to the dismay of the crown prince, Liu Qi. Some accounts say that later the emperor demanded Liu Qi perform the same act of devotion, sucking at the boils as Deng Tong had. As expected, the prince gagged, recoiled, and vomited. This response not only infuriated Emperor Wen but revealed that none could ever be as loyal as Deng Tong. As for the crown prince, this was a humiliation he would never forget.

And so, when Emperor Wen died, Deng Tong's world collapsed. Liu Qi, now sitting on the throne as Emperor Jing, worked fast to curb Deng Tong's influence. He stripped his father's favorite of his wealth and accused him of illegal dealings. No longer protected by imperial affection, Deng Tong was a step closer to his demise. The fortune teller's prophecy came true after all. Deng Tong, once one of the richest men in China and the intimate favorite of an emperor, starved to death in poverty.

Chapter 8 – Love and Demise

There once lived a wealthy family in Shangyu. They had just welcomed a child. Named Zhu Yingtai, she was the only daughter among nine brothers. Her life was perfect. She was cherished by her parents and fortunate to have been born into an upper-class family. Yingtai, however, was unlike any other young girl. She was always intrigued by knowledge. She could memorize the classics recited by her brothers and would often ask questions beyond her years. Over time, Yingtai grew a desire to study properly. Yet, even if women lived in a privileged environment, they were often denied such opportunities. Girls were trained for weaving, music, and the duties of the household. To seek scholarly learning, to sit beside men in the lecture halls, was forbidden.

Even though she knew this was the norm for everyone who shared her gender, Yingtai never planned to abandon her hunger for knowledge. Every day, she would plead to her parents to allow her to study in Hangzhou, and each day, they firmly said no. One day, Yingtai dressed herself in her brothers' clothes. She tied her hair neatly into a scholar's knot and donned the robes of a young man. Once more, she confronted her parents. This time around, her parents relented to her wish, but with one condition: she was to keep her true gender a secret.

A monument of Zhu Yingtai and Liang Shanbo in Verona, Italy.[26]

Yingtai was ecstatic. Almost immediately, she prepared herself for the journey to Hangzhou. On her way, she met a fellow scholar. He introduced himself as Liang Shanbo. Unlike Yingtai, who grew up in a wealthy family, Shanbo was born into a rather modest family. Although not swimming in wealth, he was often described as earnest and kind; some even summarized his character as a man of quiet virtue. Once the disguised Yingtai discovered that Shanbo was heading to the same destination, Yingtai invited him to travel together. Within minutes of their first meeting, the two clicked, falling into easy conversation. It was as if their bond was meant to be. By the time they reached Hangzhou, the two had grown so close that they swore to become study mates.

The two studied in Hangzhou for three years, and Shanbo never discovered Yingtai's true gender. Still, it was as if they were glued to each other. In the morning, they would study books, sitting side by side. When afternoon came, they recited passages. In the evening, the two could often be seen walking the fields, discussing topics like virtue and fate. It is safe to say that Yingtai matched Shanbo in wit and insight. While Shanbo saw Yingtai as the truest companion (or brother) he had ever known, Yingtai began to develop feelings for him. She would occasionally drop hints, speaking of mandarin ducks that never live apart, but Shanbo never understood. There were times when he poked fun at Yingtai for comparing herself to a woman.

One day, Yingtai received a letter from her parents, summoning her home. This was the moment when things changed. She did not want to leave the love of her life, but at the same time, she could not ignore her parents. She prepared to leave Hangzhou and said her goodbyes. Of course, the farewell weighed heavily upon her. Shanbo felt the same. Unwilling to part so soon, he decided to walk with her for eighteen miles beyond the city walls. Again, Yingtai tried to subtly reveal her secret, telling Shanbo that she was not what she seemed. And yet again, Shanbo failed to grasp her meaning, replying with only a warm smile. At last, Yingtai decided to tell him that she had another sister who was beautiful and unwed. She encouraged Shanbo to visit her family one day and promised that she herself would arrange a union between him and her sister. Shanbo was perplexed by the request but promised to visit regardless.

When Yingtai returned home, her secret life ended. She put away the robes she had worn in Hangzhou, unbound her hair, and continued her duty as a daughter. Then came her parents, who informed her of the reason behind the sudden callback. As it turned out, they had already promised her hand to a wealthy man named Ma Wencai. Yingtai's heart was crushed. She begged her parents to break the match.

"My heart belongs to another," she may have said. Yet, their answer was final. After all, to cancel a promised marriage was to bring embarrassment to the family. And so, a marriage ceremony was set in motion.

Shanbo, on the other hand, tried to live his life as a scholar as usual. However, it was different without Yingtai. This was when he remembered his promise. Shanbo then journeyed to Yingtai's house, hoping to see his study mate once more and perhaps meet the mysterious sister that Yingtai had spoken about.

When he arrived at the door, it was Yingtai (without her disguise) who greeted him. Just by looking into her eyes, Shanbo finally understood the hints that Yingtai occasionally threw at him. Joy struck him, knowing that the sister was Zhu Yingtai herself, his beloved companion from those years of study. Shanbo confessed his love right there and then, and Yingtai returned it. However, their fate was already bound by her parents' decision.

When Yingtai informed him that she was to be married to another man, Shanbo's world turned dark. He returned home in despair. Grief consumed him to the point he fell seriously ill. His strength failed, and within weeks, he died with Yingtai's name still carved in his heart.

When news of her true love's death reached her ears, Yingtai could feel sorrow overtaking her entire being. Yet, there was nothing she could do. Her wedding to Ma Wencai was still on schedule. She did, however, request that her bridal procession pass by Liang Shanbo's grave. Her parents, thinking the request harmless, agreed.

When the day finally came, Yingtai found her hands trembling within her sleeves. As promised, the procession wound its way through the countryside until it reached Liang's resting place. As they drew near, a fierce wind suddenly blew. The horses reared and refused to press on despite the attendants' pressuring. Yingtai, knowing that it was a sign by the heavenly gods, leapt from her carriage. She stripped off her fiery red wedding garments, revealing beneath them the white cloth of mourning. She made haste to Shanbo's grave, where she dropped to her knees. There, the bride-to-be wept continuously.

The winds howled louder, this time accompanied by lightning that appeared as if it was splitting the heavens. Suddenly, the grave split open, and without hesitation, Yingtai threw herself into the dark chasm. Before anyone could get close to the grave, the earth closed again, sealing the two lovers together, forever.

Later, when the sky calmed down and the thunder and lightning were no more, the sun began shining over the land. Several farmers soon noticed two small butterflies fluttering from the grave.

Meng Jiangnü's Grief

This story took place during the Qin dynasty. It involved a young woman who went by the name of Meng Jiangnü. Legend has it that she belonged to a family that was neither rich nor powerful. Her kindness, beauty, and gentle nature, however, were her most precious traits and often captivated the hearts of the people around her.

Meng Jiangnü lived in a quaint village where she spent her days tending to her family and garden. One evening, as Jiangnü was admiring the autumn leaves, she heard a faint rustling noise coming from a bush. Curious, the young woman went and checked to see what made the sound. Perhaps it was a cat or a squirrel, she may have thought to herself. The closer she got to the bush, the more Jiangnü's heart began to race. Turns out, the noise came from a man hiding in the bush. Panicked, Jiangnü called for her parents. The man, afraid that she would cause a commotion, jumped out and explained his circumstances.

His name was Fan Qiliang, and he was hiding from the government officials. This was a time when the emperor, Qin Shi Huang, demanded endless labor from his subjects to build his grand wall. It did not matter whether they were willing to contribute; many were seized from their homes and forced into the construction work. They had to work regardless of the weather or even their health. As a result, many ended up perishing from hunger, cold, and exhaustion. Hence, it made sense for Fan Qiliang to run away, hoping he could escape this daunting fate.

Having heard his reasoning, Meng Jiangnü grew sympathetic. Instead of turning him in, she offered the man refuge. She brought him food and water, treating him like a guest. In time, her kindness blossomed into love, and the two were married. For a short while, it seemed like their lives were filled with joy. However, happiness was fragile under Qin rule. In just a matter of days following their wedding, government officials came to the village, searching for more able-bodied men. Fan Qiliang was eventually discovered and dragged away, taken to labor on the Great Wall. Meng Jiangnü could only stand and watch, powerless to stop the soldiers.

Meng Jiangnü patiently waited for the return of her husband, praying each night for his safety. Weeks turned into long months, yet not a single letter arrived from Fan Qiliang. She asked around one day, hoping someone had heard news of her husband, but unfortunately, she returned home empty-handed. That night, Meng Jiangnü had a dream. In it, she saw Fan Qilian shaking and trembling as he worked without rest in the cold winter weather. Worried that her husband might be in trouble, Meng Jiangnü sewed warm clothes, packed food, and began the long journey northward, determined to find her husband.

The road was harsh, and the journey long. She crossed rivers, climbed hills, and braved cold winds. She tirelessly asked every passerby if they had seen Fan Qiliang among the laborers. Many shook their heads. At last, she reached the construction site. There, she was able to witness first-hand the place of misery and despair so many men were terrified of. Thousands of men toiled under the lash of overseers, their faces hollow with hunger and their hands bloodied from lifting stones. Indeed, the wall rose high and wide, but beneath its stones also lay countless bones of those who had died from exhaustion.

Meng Jiangnü searched desperately, asking each worker if they knew of her husband. When the sky had almost lost its light, Meng Jiangnü finally got her answer, though it was far from what she wanted to hear. One of the laborers told her that Fan Qiliang had perished a few weeks prior. His body was buried within the very wall he had been forced to build.

An illustration of Meng Jiagnü weeping before the Great Wall.[37]

Meng Jiangnü was left speechless. She could not feel her body. She fell to her knees before the towering wall, still clutching the winter clothes she had sewn for her beloved husband. She remained at the foot of the wall for days, crying continuously. Legend has it that her sorrow was so deep that it moved even the gods. Her cries grew more piercing as the days went by, until one day the earth responded with a tremble. A thunderous crack echoed through the land as a section of the Great Wall collapsed. From within this rubble, the remains of Fan Qilian were revealed.

The destruction angered the emperor, who came to the site so he could punish Meng Jiangnü. However, the moment he laid eyes on her, the emperor was starstruck; he had never seen a woman as beautiful as her. Hence, instead of punishing her, the emperor proposed marriage. Meng Jiangnü, her cheeks still wet with tears, reluctantly agreed, but only if the emperor allowed her to provide a proper burial for Fan Qiliang. To this, the emperor agreed.

She gathered his bones one by one with her trembling hands and buried her husband. But could she bring herself to marry the emperor? How could she when her heart belonged to Fan Qiliang and the emperor was the reason he died? When the burial ceremony was done, Meng Jiangnü requested the emperor to fulfil another one of her wishes: to visit the ocean. It was clear that her heart was broken beyond repair. The moment she got on a ship with the emperor, Meng Jiangnü threw herself into the sea, her body quickly devoured by the waves.

The Ups and Downs of Love

Sima Xiangru is said to have been born in 179 BCE at the dawn of Emperor Wen's reign. Since he was born into a family of some wealth in Chengdu, Xiangru enjoyed a fine education. He was indeed a lover of literature. Even from a young age, he often immersed himself in books, mastering the classics and sharpening his prose. He also received training in the realm of music, mastering the lute to the point that every melody he plucked could stir both the heart and mind of anyone nearby. Of course, poetry and music were not the only fields he was well versed in. Xiangru also studied the art of war, eventually growing up to be a respectable swordsman known for his discipline and agility.

This combination—moderate health, immense knowledge, and exceptional martial ability—undoubtedly made him popular. He later got the attention of Emperor Jing of Han, who sat on the throne between 157 and 141 BCE. Impressed by his complete set of skills, the emperor welcomed the young man into his service. In court, Sima Xiangru was made one of the emperor's personal guards. Although this position gave him stability and standing, it brought him little joy. He preferred art, philosophy, and music to guarding the Son of Heaven. After all, according to the historian Sima Qian, Emperor Jing had little taste for literature.

And so, Xiangru began to look elsewhere, hoping he could attain fulfillment in his life. His opportunity soon arrived when Prince Xiao of Liang came to the imperial capital. He was accompanied by an entourage of not only scholars but also a band of talented musicians and rhetoricians. Their brilliance immediately captivated Xiangru. In their company, the young man got a taste of a life full of refinement, discourse, and artistry—a life that he longed for. Therefore, he made up his mind: Xiangru chose to leave his post as a guard and follow the prince to Liang.

At Prince Xiao's court, Xiangru was surrounded by great minds, giving him a chance to hone his rhetoric, improvise his verse, and perfect his melodies. Liang was indeed a melting pot of men with talent, so it was not surprising that Xiangru was able to flourish in its halls. He remained here for years, and his reputation grew steadily across the land. Things only changed in 144 BCE, when Prince Xiao died. Without his patron, Xiangru was left with no choice but to return to Chengdu. Upon his return, more bad news came. In his absence, his family fortunes had greatly withered.

With wealth and comfort at home a thing of the past, Xiangru made his way to Linqiong. He was hoping to meet with a friend who served the city as a magistrate. Since Xiangru already had influence—due to his poetry and his life as a courtier of princes—it was not hard for him to settle in. In Linqiong, he was treated with respect. His name drew the attention of the local elite. Families of influence vied for his company, inviting him to banquets and seeking the honor of his presence at their tables.

One rather wealthy merchant, Zhuo Wangsun, once hosted a lavish feast and invited the poet as his honorable guest. It was one of the grandest events in Linqiong, attended by the most prominent members of the district. They indulged in endless food and flowing wine and spent the evening socializing with each other. Xiangru, however, had his attention elsewhere. He had caught sight of a certain Zhuo Wenjun, the daughter of the host.

Wenjun was well known in the district not only for being the daughter of Linqiong's well-respected merchant but also for her extraordinary beauty and refinement. She had once been married, but not for long; her husband died within a year of their union. Hence, she returned to her father, living within his household once more. Like father, like daughter, Wenjun too was a lover of music and arts. Unsurprisingly, when she heard the tunes coming from the lute played by Sima Xiangru that night—he was purposely plucking the finest melody to attract her attention—Wenjun immediately fell in love.

And so, she made her choice. She fled her father's house and eloped with the talented poet. Their union shocked the entire district. Indeed, Xiangru was popular, but he was not above or at least at the same social level as Zhuo Wangsun, whose vast fortune and influence far outweighed the poet's modest means. Wenju's decision to elope so enraged her father that he stripped her of his wealth. Hence, the couple lived their early days together full of hardship.

Still, their love prevailed. Wenjun worked alongside her husband to survive. They opened a small business selling wine in the market. Some whispered scorn, mocking the fallen daughter of Zhuo Wangsun. Yet, the two never took these cruel remarks to heart. Her father, on the other hand, grew restless with the gossip. He was embarrassed to see his daughter, once dressed in fine silks, now dressed like a commoner and working in a mere tavern. So, he relented. He restored part of Wenjun's dowry, sending servants, wealth, and resources to the couple. From then on, their lives grew easier, and with leisure restored, Sima Xiangru devoted himself once more to literature.

Again, Sima Xiangru's name reached the highest circles, and he eventually caught the attention of Emperor Wu, who succeeded Emperor Jing in 141 BCE. A man of literature and art himself, the emperor summoned Xiangru to his court. The poet dazzled with his compositions, such as the "Shanglin Fu," a long descriptive poem that captured the natural beauty of a royal hunting park, Shanglin Park.

True, Xiangru's reputation grew tremendously, but success also carried temptation with it. At court, he was surrounded by luxury and praise. He began to drift from the humble devotion that had bound him to Wenjun. Days stretched into weeks, then months. Wenjun waited in Linqiong, expecting news that her husband would bring her to the capital. Sadly, none came.

One day, a letter arrived. It contained only thirteen characters. In it, Sima Xiangru coldly confessed his intent to take a concubine, as was common among men of his current standing. The letter broke Wenjun.

However, she chose not to unleash wrath. Neither did she beg desperately for his compassion. Instead, she crafted a poem known as "Yuanlang Shi" (Blaming My Husband). In the verses, she poured out her grief, expressed beautifully the betrayal that she felt, and wrote the remembrance of all they had shared. She reminded him of the night she fled her father's house, the years of poverty endured at his side, the scorn she had borne willingly for love. She did not throw bitter insults but rather piercing honesty. Later, she followed with another poem named "Baitou Yin" (Song of White Hair), in which she talked about how love is fragile, just as beauty and youth.

When Sima Xiangru read her words, shame engulfed him. The woman who had risked everything for him, who had labored beside him when he was penniless, now humbled him with poetry that revealed his betrayal. He chose to abandon his intention to take a concubine and returned to Wenjun. In the end, the two lived together until death.

The Broken Emperor

Emperor Xuanzong of Tang first came to power in 712 CE. He reigned wisely, guided by trustworthy ministers, and presided over what scholars later called the Kaiyuan Golden Age. But as the years passed and his youth faded, so did his interest in the serious duties of governing. He had also lost his other half, the consort Lady Wu. The emperor longed for companionship, but it was not easy to find someone who could check all the lists.

That was, however, until he laid eyes on Yang Yuhuan. She was young, only nineteen, with radiant skin, delicate features, and eyes that seemed to sparkle with mischief and life. Her beauty was beyond the world; some claim she had a face that would shame even the prettiest flower on earth. History, too, would remember her as one of the Four Great Beauties of China. However, there was an obstacle to Xuanzong claiming her for his own: she had already been married to his son, Li Mao.

Still, the smitten emperor could not erase his feelings. Yet how could the ruler of the mighty Tang dynasty openly take his own daughter-in-law without scandal? If he did so, it would certainly be a blow to imperial prestige. But Xuanzong came up with a plan. He told his son to pressure Yang Yuhuan into walking the path of religion. As a result, Yang Yuhuan became a Taoist nun, severing her marriage. Outwardly, she became "Lady of the Dao," her hair bound and her days devoted to prayer. But, under the cover of night, she would slip into disguises and meet the emperor. This, however, was an open secret. But she lived this double life for seven years.

When Li Mao eventually remarried, Xuanzong wasted no time. He summoned Yang Yuhuan back into the palace and gave her the title *guifei*, or "noble consort," which was the emperor's favorite. From then on, Yang Guifei became the center of his world.

Yang Guifei enjoyed this new level of prestige. She used this opportunity to lift her family's fortune. She showered his brothers and sisters with wealth and lands. Her cousin, Yang Guozhong, was also elevated to the position of prime minister, one of the most powerful offices in the empire. But many viewed Tang Guozhong as unfit for the role. Not only was he clumsy, but he was also corrupt in politics. This incompetence slowly poisoned the government and sowed seeds of resentment. Although these seeds of nepotism would one day turn into a calamity, none dared to speak up.

Yang Guifei mounting a horse.[28]

Yang Guifei herself lived a life of extraordinary luxury. Her wardrobe was filled with nothing but the most exquisite silks dyed in the rarest colors. Each of them was typically embroidered with phoenixes and peonies, two of the most favorite motifs among the nobles. Hundreds of maids also attended to her every step, and the emperor would move heaven and earth to satisfy her cravings. According to one story, Guifei loved lychees. This fruit, however, could only grow in fields far from the capital. So, to please her, the emperor ordered his officials to travel far, just so they could source the fruit. For weeks, horses and couriers raced across provinces, carrying the precious fruit at full speed so that the emperor's dearest consort could enjoy it fresh. The scramble left ministers grumbling about the absurdity of palace priorities, but no one dared speak too loudly, especially against the emperor's favorite.

Emperor Xuanzong and his favorite, Yang Guifei.[39]

Beauty was not her only strong suit. Yang Guifei was also bestowed with a gift for music and dance. She often composed songs for Xuanzong. She played the pipa and flute and performed graceful dances in the palace halls. The emperor could watch her for hours, getting so entranced that he would forget the affairs of the empire.

Of course, like any other love story, theirs was not without quarrels. Yang Guifei was described as fiercely jealous. It was difficult for her to tolerate those who gained the emperor's affection. Once, after a bitter quarrel, Xuanzong banished her to her cousin's home in disgrace. But the emperor could not bear to live a life without his favorite consort and soon sent for her to return. Another episode of banishment came a few years later. This time, it was due to the consort's alleged theft of a flute. Again, the banishment did not last long.

Knowing that the emperor held a soft spot for Yang Guifei in his heart, many courtiers began to realize that their path to heightened influence lay through her. They knew that those who pleased Yang Guifei could win the emperor's ear. Thus, these nobles showered the consort with gifts and flattery. The one who excelled at this was a general who commanded the armies on the northern frontier. His name was An Lushan, and his charming personality sat so well with the consort that she was said to have jokingly referred to him as her adopted son. Little did she know that An Lushan was the key to her demise.

The general had ambition to sit on the throne, so in 755 CE, he led a rebellion. His armies marched with terrifying speed, seizing cities and threatening even Chang'an. Panic swept the court. Even Xuanzong and his entourage fled westward, seeking refuge in the mountains of Sichuan. Things took a dark turn for the emperor and his consort along the road at Mawei. There, the imperial guards, who had grown extremely exhausted and furious, turned their anger toward the emperor's favorites. They slew Yang Guozhong, blaming him for corruption and misrule. Then, they pointed their fingers at Yang Guifei, demanding her execution.

The emperor was torn. He pleaded and wept, but his soldiers stood unmoved. They would go no further unless she was gone. At last, Xuanzong relented. Yang Guifei was led beneath the trees of a wayside Buddhist shrine. There, she was strangled with a silken cord. The emperor's beloved, the woman for whom he had bent the empire, now lay lifeless on the earth.

The emperor lived, but he was a broken man, beyond fixing. Though the Tang armies eventually crushed An Lushan's rebellion under the leadership of Xuanzong's son (who ruled as Emperor Suzong), the dynasty never fully recovered its former strength.

Conclusion

Looking at China today, it is easy to assume that its story has always been one of unstoppable power. The truth, however, is different. China's history is anything but steady. It is named the world's oldest continuous civilization not because it was unshakable but because it was constantly being shaken—and rebuilt over and over again.

Across these short pages, we have saw dynasties rise and fall, sometimes spectacularly. Famines and rebellions were recurring themes of Chinese history. Cities that once became a melting pot of merchants and scholars were never guaranteed endurance; Loulan, for one, eventually vanished into the desert despite being one of the most precious centers fought over by major powers. Entire cultures, such as Sanxingdui, left us with more questions than answers about their story and disappearance despite leaving behind dozens of impressive artifacts. Even the great Han dynasty faltered, paving the way for ancient China to eventually fracture yet again. Indeed, continuity was never promised. But China survived only because of the people—both named and unnamed—who never failed to pick up the pieces and carry them forward.

Of course, it was not only the Son of Heaven who held the line. There were many others who contributed to the civilization's survival. While emperors and dynasties gave their names to eras, it was often generals on the frontier, scholars in their studies, poets in exile, and even women in the palace who kept the thread of continuity from snapping. Shangguan Wan'er and Princess Pingyang, for instance, went against the norms of a patriarchal society; one used her expertise in words to see to matters of the state while the other raised an entire army as part of a rebellion. There were also those like Wu Qi and Tan Daoji, who led the empire to triumph yet were rewarded with tragedy and injustice. Love stories in ancient China likewise had themes of tragedy and misfortune woven into the plot.

It is clear that China's endurance came not from being unshakable but from being resilient. Continuity lived in forgotten cities, in overshadowed rebellions, and even in poems written by kidnapped victims. Vulnerability was always a part of the nation's long history, and so was the will to start again. True, the stories were not always glorious, but they were always human. That is why these forgotten voices and overlooked episodes matter. They fill in the spaces between the grand narratives and remind us that history is not only the story of emperors but of people.

Here's another book by Matt Clayton that you might like

Free Bonus from Captivating History (Available for a Limited time)

Hi History Lovers!

Now you have a chance to join our exclusive history list so you can get your first history ebook for free as well as discounts and a potential to get more history books for free!

Simply visit the link below to join.

Or, Scan the QR code!

captivatinghistory.com/ebook

Also, make sure to follow us on Facebook, X, and YouTube by searching for Captivating History.

Bibliography

"Ban Zhao." The University of Chicago, February 2, 2022.
womanisrational.uchicago.edu/2022/02/02/ban-zhao.

"Brave Men Never Return: On the Historical Trail of Assassin Jing Ke." The Hutong.
thehutong.com/brave-men-never-return-on-the-historical-trail-of-assassin-jing-ke.
Accessed August 18, 2025.

"Bronze Sacred Tree Found in Sanxingdui Sacrificial Pit." *The History Blog*,
September 9, 2021. www.thehistoryblog.com/archives/62185.

"Cai Lun - Improving Papermaking Technology." Chinese Learning, January 12,
2023. www.chineselearning.com/chinese-name/cai-lun-papermaking.

Cartwright, Mark. "Eunuchs in Ancient China." *World History*, July 27, 2017.
www.worldhistory.org/article/1109/eunuchs-in-ancient-china.

Cartwright, Mark. "Women in Ancient China." *World History*, October 19, 2017.
www.worldhistory.org/article/1136/women-in-ancient-china.

Clementine. "Ban Chao: A Diplomatic Legend on the China Silk Road." China Xian
Tour, updated March 6, 2025.
www.chinaxiantour.com/xian-travel-blog/ban-chao.html.

Colville, Alex. "China's Renaissance Man." The China Project, March 1, 2021.
www.thechinaproject.com/2021/03/01/chinas-renaissance-man.

Colville, Alex. "Yu The Great, Tamer of China's Greatest Floods." The China Project, August 24, 2020.
www.thechinaproject.com/2020/08/24/yu-the-great-tamer-of-chinas-greatest-floods.

Ghose, Tia. "Mystery of Ancient Chinese Civilization's Disappearance Explained."
Live Science, December 24, 2014.
www.livescience.com/49247-chinese-civilization-disappearance-explained.html.

"How Was the Ancient Loulan City Discovered?" Silk Road Travel, June 22, 2020.
www.silkroadtravel.com/silk-road-travel-guide/ancient-city-loulan.html.

"Inside the Elegant Concubine Rankings of the Six Palaces of the Tang Dynasty Imperial Harem." Amimisu, YouTube, July 17, 2025.
www.youtube.com/watch?v=21V0qcBBKeQ&t=983s.

Jin, Alex. "Why Did Emperor Qin Shi Huang Not Determine the Empress?" Travel
China Guide, August 4, 2025.
www.travelchinaguide.com/attraction/shaanxi/xian/terra_cotta_army/qin-shihuang-empress.htm?srsltid=AfmBOoql3JkadV9tVAhpgTcPY-_HUFOT5X5k2lPxWiyIwLHOtffO5yEU.

Leung, Crystal. "Gay Emperors in Chinese History." China Publishing Group, June
27, 2019. www.theworldofchinese.com/2019/06/gay-emperors-in-chinese-history.

London, Helen. "Zhuo Wenjun, the Woman Who Got Her Man Back with the Beauty
of Poems." *Nspirement,* September 6, 2022.
www.nspirement.com/2022/09/06/zhuo-wenjun-poems.html.

Mark, Emily. "Xia Dynasty." *World History,* January 16, 2016.
www.worldhistory.org/Xia_Dynasty.

Mark, Joshua. J. "Sima Qian." *World History,* July 6, 2020.
www.worldhistory.org/Sima_Qian.

Norman, Jeremy. "The First Emperor of China Destroys Most Records of the Past
Along with 460 or More, Scholars." Norman Jeremy. Accessed August 13, 2025. www.historyofinformation.com/detail.php?id=2491.

"Princess Pingyang Co-Founder of Tang Dynasty." Cool History Bros, YouTube,

December 26, 2020. www.youtube.com/watch?v=Nt-nqgXoiM8.

Ryan. "Zhu Yingtai and Liang Shanbo – a Relentless Love in China's Folklore."

China Partnership, February 12, 2015. www.chinapartnership.org/blog/2015/02/zhu-yingtai-and-liang-shanbo-a-relentless-love-in-chinas-folklore.

"Shocking Romance of Male Concubines in the Han Dynasty of Ancient China."

Amimisu, YouTube, July 24, 2025. www.youtube.com/watch?v=WMCl-4SKjbs.

Stewart, James. "Li Yannian, House of Flying Daggers." Vermont Public, September

30, 2019. www.vermontpublic.org/programs/2019-09-30/timeline-li-yannian-house-of-flying-daggers.

"The Lost Kingdom of Loulan." Gwong Zau Kung Fu, May 10, 2021, www.gwongzaukungfu.com/en/the-lost-kingdom-of-loulan.

"The Lost World of Sanxingdui." *World Archaeology*, November 23, 2023. www.world-archaeology.com/features/the-lost-world-of-sanxingdui.

"The Musical Love Story of Sima Xiangru and Zhuo Wenjun." The Historian Hut,

March 31, 2020. www.thehistorianshut.com/2020/03/31/the-musical-love-story-of-sima-xiangru-and-zhuo-wenjun.

"The Mysterious History of Ancient China's Nine Tripod Cauldrons." History Skills, Accessed August 22, 2025.

www.historyskills.com/classroom/year-7/nine-tripod-cauldrons/?srsltid=AfmBOoriV64qLks-dRGV6wP69tpJPp8AAasAafFQN1E0QOSpugpqtWEZ.

Theobald, Ulrich. "Wu Zixu." Theobold Ulrich, November 13, 2010. www.chinaknowledge.de/History/Zhou/personswuzixu.html.

Wee, Kek Koon. "Qu Yuan, Chinese Patriot Whose Death Is Said to Have Inspired

Dragon Boat Festival Customs." *South China Morning Post*, May 31, 2025. www.scmp.com/lifestyle/chinese-culture/article/3312392/qu-yuan-chinese-patriot-whose-death-said-have-inspired-dragon-boat-festival-customs.

Wong, Noel. "How a Legendary Romance Ended China's Golden Age." *Free Malaysia Today*, February 15, 2022. www.freemalaysiatoday.com/category/leisure/2022/02/15/how-a-legendary-romance-ended-chinas-golden-age.

Wu, Haiyun, and Ruolin Ye. "The Mysterious Ancient City That's Rewriting Chinese
History." *Sixth Tone*, July 7, 2021. www.sixthtone.com/news/1007903.
Xinhua. "Exploring the Lost Land of Loulan." *China Daily*, April 22, 2024.
www.chinadailyhk.com/hk/article/581516.
"Xuanwu Gate Incident - Tang Taizong's Bloody Rise to Power." Cool History Bros,
YouTube, January 5, 2021. www.youtube.com/watch?v=9gbSgtztHA8.
"Zhuo Wenjun: A Tale of Love and Betrayal." Kim Dramer, YouTube,
January 1, 2021. www.youtube.com/watch?v=R_dV3gER2aI.

Image Sources

1   Pravit, CC BY-SA 4.0 <https://creativecommons.org/licenses/by-sa/4.0>, via Wikimedia Commons: https://commons.wikimedia.org /wiki/File:Taklamakan_desert.jpg

2   Schreiber, CC BY-SA 3.0 <http://creativecommons.org/licenses/by-sa/3.0/>, via Wikimedia Commons: https://commons.wikimedia.org/wiki/File: Tarimbecken_3._Jahrhundert.png

3   No machine-readable author provided. World Imaging assumed (based on copyright claims)., CC BY-SA 3.0 <http://creativecommons.org/licenses/by-sa/3.0/>, via Wikimedia Commons: https://commons.wikimedia.org/wiki/File: LoulanCarvedWoodenBeam.JPG

4   Dan LundbergEric Feng, CC BY-SA 4.0 <https://creativecommons.org/licenses/by-sa/4.0>, via Wikimedia Commons: https://commons.wikimedia.org /wiki/File:Beauty_of_Loulan_(reconstruction_and_original).jpg

5   Tyg728, CC BY-SA 4.0 <https://creativecommons.org/licenses/by-sa/4.0>, via Wikimedia Commons: https://commons.wikimedia.org/wiki/File :%E2%85%A0%E5%8F%B7%E5%A4%A7%E5%9E%8B%E9%9D%92%E9%93%9 C%E7%A5%9E%E6%A0%91.jpg

6   Tyg728, CC BY-SA 4.0 <https://creativecommons.org/licenses/by-sa/4.0>, via Wikimedia Commons: https://commons.wikimedia.org/wiki/File:%E9%9 D%92%E9%93%9C%E7%BA%B5%E7%9B%AE%E9%9D%A2%E5%85%B7B.jpg

7   Gary Todd, CC0, via Wikimedia Commons: https://commons.wikimedia.org/wiki/File:2014_Jinsha_Gold_Mask_a.jpg

8   John Hill, CC BY-SA 3.0 <https://creativecommons.org/licenses/by-sa/3.0>, via Wikimedia Commons: https://commons.wikimedia.org/wiki/File: Statue_commemorating_Ban_Chao,_Kashgar.jpg

9 歷代聖賢半身像 冊 檀道濟, CC BY 4.0
   <https://creativecommons.org/licenses/by/4.0>, via Wikimedia Commons:
   https://commons.wikimedia.org/wiki/File:%E6%AD%B7%E4%BB%A3%E8%81%9
   6%E8%B3%A2%E5%8D%8A%E8%BA%AB%E5%83%8F_%E5%86%8A_%E6%
   AA%80%E9%81%93%E6%BF%9F_(Tan_Daoji).png

10 en:user: Kowloonese, CC BY-SA 3.0 <http://creativecommons.org/licenses/by-
   sa/3.0/>, via Wikimedia Commons:
   https://commons.wikimedia.org/wiki/File:EastHanSeismograph.JPG

11 https://commons.wikimedia.org/wiki/File:Letter_on_Papyrus.jpg

12 https://commons.wikimedia.org/wiki/File:Jingangjing.jpg

13 Gary Todd, CC0, via Wikimedia Commons:
   https://commons.wikimedia.org/wiki/File:Fu_Hao_Tomb,_c._1200_BC,_Reign_of
   _King_Wu_Ding,_Shang_Dynasty_3.jpg

14 https://commons.wikimedia.org/wiki/File:Ban_Zhao_-
   _Wushuang_Pu_(pref_1690,_1961).jpg

15 https://commons.wikimedia.org/wiki/File:%E7%95%AB%E9%BA%97%E7
   %8F%A0%E8%90%83%E7%A7%80_Gathering_Gems_of_Beauty_(%E6%BC%A2
   %E8%94%A1%E6%96%87%E5%A7%AC)_2.jpg

16 https://commons.wikimedia.org/wiki/File:Assassination_attempt_on_Qin_
   Shi_Huang.jpg

17 SY, CC BY-SA 4.0 <https://creativecommons.org/licenses/by-sa/4.0>, via
   Wikimedia Commons: https://commons.wikimedia.org/wiki/File:
   Nine_Provinces_of_China.png

18 https://commons.wikimedia.org/wiki/File:La_expedici%C3%B3n_de_
   Xu_Fu,_por_Utagawa_Kuniyoshi.jpg

19 Metropolitan Museum of Art, CC0, via Wikimedia Commons:
   https://commons.wikimedia.org/wiki/File:%E5%85%83_%E4%BD%9A%E5%90%8
   D_%E5%80%A3%E8%B6%99%E5%AD%9F%E9%A0%AB_%E4%B9%9D%E6%
   AD%8C%E5%9C%96_%E5%86%8A-Nine_Songs_MET_DP375119.jpg

20 vlasta2, bluefootedbooby on flickr.com, CC BY 2.0
   <https://creativecommons.org/licenses/by/2.0>, via Wikimedia Commons:
   https://commons.wikimedia.org/wiki/File:Bamboo_book_-_binding_-_UCR.jpg

21 https://commons.wikimedia.org/wiki/File:Sima_Qian_(painted_portrait).jpg

22 dayu490301, CC BY 3.0 <https://creativecommons.org/licenses/by/3.0>, via
   Wikimedia Commons: https://commons.wikimedia.org/wiki/File:
   %E5%8F%B8%E9%A9%AC%E8%BF%81%E5%A2%93_-_panoramio.jpg

23 陈文 https://www.flickr.com/people/univers-finder/, CC BY 2.0
   <https://creativecommons.org/licenses/by/2.0>, via Wikimedia Commons:
   https://commons.wikimedia.org/wiki/File:Wang_Zhaojun_Peking_Opera_13.jpg

24 https://commons.wikimedia.org/wiki/File:%E6%BC%A2%E6%AD%A6%
   E5%B8%9D.jpg

25 https://commons.wikimedia.org/wiki/File:%E7%95%AB%E9%BA%97%E7%8F%A0%E8%90%83%E7%A7%80_Gathering_Gems_of_Beauty_(%E6%BC%A2%E6%9D%8E%E5%A4%AB%E4%BA%BA)_2.jpg

26 Andrijko Z., CC BY-SA 4.0 <https://creativecommons.org/licenses/by-sa/4.0>, via Wikimedia Commons: https://commons.wikimedia.org/wiki/File:Monument_to_Liang_Shanbo_and_Zhu_Yingtai_near_the_Tombe_di_Giulietta_in_Verona,_Italy.jpg

27 https://commons.wikimedia.org/wiki/File:Meng_Jiang_Nu_Song_Dynasty_Lie_Nu_Zhuan.jpg

28 https://commons.wikimedia.org/wiki/File:Ch%27ien_Hs%C3%BCan_002.jpg

29 https://commons.wikimedia.org/wiki/File:Kano_Eitoku_007.jpg